MznLnx

Missing Links Exam Preps

Exam Prep for

E-Business and E-Commerce Management

Chaffey, 3rd Edition

The MznLnx Exam Prep is your link from the texbook and lecture to your exams.
The MznLnx Exam Preps are unauthorized and comprehensive reviews of your textbooks.

All material provided by MznLnx and Rico Publications (c) 2010
Textbook publishers and textbook authors do not particpate in or contribute to these reviews.

MznLnx

Rico Publications

Exam Prep for E-Business and E-Commerce Management
3rd Edition
Chaffey

Publisher: Raymond Houge
Assistant Editor: Michael Rouger
Text and Cover Designer: Lisa Buckner
Marketing Manager: Sara Swagger
Project Manager, Editorial Production: Jerry Emerson
Art Director: Vernon Lowerui

Product Manager: Dave Mason
Editorial Assitant: Rachel Guzmanji
Pedagogy: Debra Long
Cover Image: Jim Reed/Getty Images
Text and Cover Printer: City Printing, Inc.
Compositor: Media Mix, Inc.

(c) 2010 Rico Publications
ALL RIGHTS RESERVED. No part of this work covered by the copyright may be reproduced or used in any form or by an means--graphic, electronic, or mechanical, including photocopying, recording, taping, Web distribution, information storage, and retrieval systems, or in any other manner--without the written permission of the publisher.

Printed in the United States
ISBN:

For more information about our products, contact us at:
Dave.Mason@RicoPublications.com

For permission to use material from this text or product, submit a request online to:
Dave.Mason@RicoPublications.com

Contents

CHAPTER 1
Introduction to e-business and e-commerce — 1

CHAPTER 2
E-commerce fundamentals — 7

CHAPTER 3
E-business infrastructure — 13

CHAPTER 4
E-environment — 19

CHAPTER 5
E-business strategy — 26

CHAPTER 6
Supply chain management — 37

CHAPTER 7
E-procurement — 42

CHAPTER 8
E-marketing — 44

CHAPTER 9
Customer relationship management — 52

CHAPTER 10
Change management — 58

CHAPTER 11
Analysis and design — 65

CHAPTER 12
Implementation and maintenance — 69

ANSWER KEY — 76

TO THE STUDENT

COMPREHENSIVE

The *MznLnx* Exam Prep series is designed to help you pass your exams. Editors at MznLnx review your textbooks and then prepare these practice exams to help you master the textbook material. Unlike study guides, workbooks, and practice tests provided by the texbook publisher and textbook authors, *MznLnx* gives you **all** of the material in each chapter in exam form, not just samples, so you can be sure to nail your exam.

MECHANICAL

The MznLnx Exam Prep series creates exams that will help you learn the subject matter as well as test you on your understanding. Each question is designed to help you master the concept. Just working through the exams, you gain an understanding of the subject--its a simple mechanical process that produces success.

INTEGRATED STUDY GUIDE AND REVIEW

MznLnx is not just a set of exams designed to test you, its also a comprehensive review of the subject content. Each exam question is also a review of the concept, making sure that you will get the answer correct without having to go to other sources of material. You learn as you go! Its the easiest way to pass an exam.

HUMOR

Studying can be tedious and dry. MznLnx's instructional design includes moderate humor within the exam questions on occassion, to break the tedium and revitalize the brain

Chapter 1. Introduction to e-business and e-commerce

1. In law, _____ is the term to describe a partnership between two or more parties.

In England a number of statutes on the subject have been passed, the chief being the Bastardy Act of 1845, and the Bastardy Laws Amendment Acts of 1872 and 1873. The mother of a bastard may summon the putative father to petty sessions within twelve months of the birth (or at any later time if he is proved to have contributed to the child's support within twelve months after the birth), and the justices, as after hearing evidence on both sides, may, if the mother's evidence be corroborated in some material particular, adjudge the man to be the putative father of the child, and order him to pay a sum not exceeding five shillings a week for its maintenance, together with a sum for expenses incidental to the birth, or the funeral expenses, if it has died before the date of order, and the costs of the proceedings.

   a. Adam Smith
   b. Affiliation
   c. Abraham Harold Maslow
   d. Affiliation

2. _____ consists of the processes a company uses to track and organize its contacts with its current and prospective customers. _____ software is used to support these processes; information about customers and customer interactions can be entered, stored and accessed by employees in different company departments. Typical _____ goals are to improve services provided to customers, and to use customer contact information for targeted marketing.
   a. Disruptive technology
   b. Marketing plan
   c. Green marketing
   d. Customer relationship management

3.

   _____ is a systematic method to improve the 'value' of goods or products and services by using an examination of function. Value, as defined, is the ratio of function to cost. Value can therefore be increased by either improving the function or reducing the cost.

   a. Cellular manufacturing
   b. Master production schedule
   c. Capacity planning
   d. Value engineering

4. _____ is, in very basic words, a position a firm occupies against its competitors.

According to Michael Porter, the three methods for creating a sustainable _____ are through:

1. Cost leadership

2. Differentiation

3. Focus (economics)

   a. Theory Z
   b. 1990 Clean Air Act
   c. Competitive advantage
   d. 28-hour day

5. _____, commonly referred to as 'eBusiness' or 'e-Business', may be defined as the utilization of information and communication technologies (ICT) in support of all the activities of business. Commerce constitutes the exchange of products and services between businesses, groups and individuals and hence can be seen as one of the essential activities of any business. Hence, electronic commerce or eCommerce focuses on the use of ICT to enable the external activities and relationships of the business with individuals, groups and other businesses.

   a. AAAI
   b. Electronic business
   c. A Stake in the Outcome
   d. A4e

6. In decision theory and estimation theory, the _____ of an estimator, $\hat{\theta}$, of an unknown parameter of the distribution, θ, is the expected value of the loss function

$$R(\theta, \hat{\theta}) = \mathbb{E}_\theta L(\theta, \hat{\theta}) = \int L(\theta, \hat{\theta})\, dP_\theta.$$

where dP_θ is a probability measure parametrized by θ.

- For a scalar parameter θ and a quadratic loss function,

$$L(\theta, \hat{\theta}) = (\theta - \hat{\theta})^2$$

the _____ function becomes the mean squared error of the estimate,

$$R(\theta, \hat{\theta}) = E_\theta(\theta - \hat{\theta})^2$$

- In density estimation, the unknown parameter is probability density itself. The loss function is typically chosen to be a norm in an appropriate function space. For example, for L^2 norm,

$$L(f, \hat{f}) = \|f - \hat{f}\|_2^2$$

the _____ function becomes the mean integrated squared error

$$R(f, \hat{f}) = E\|f - \hat{f}\|^2$$

a. Risk aversion
b. Linear model
c. Financial modeling
d. Risk

7. _____, commonly known as e-commerce, consists of the buying and selling of products or services over electronic systems such as the Internet and other computer networks. The amount of trade conducted electronically has grown extraordinarily with widespread Internet usage. The use of commerce is conducted in this way, spurring and drawing on innovations in electronic funds transfer, supply chain management, Internet marketing, online transaction processing, electronic data interchange (EDI), inventory management systems, and automated data collection systems.
  a. A Stake in the Outcome
  b. Online shopping
  c. A4e
  d. Electronic Commerce

8. _____ is an advertisement in which a particular product specifically mentions a competitor by name for the express purpose of showing why the competitor is inferior to the product naming it.

Chapter 1. Introduction to e-business and e-commerce

This should not be confused with parody advertisements, where a fictional product is being advertised for the purpose of poking fun at the particular advertisement, nor should it be confused with the use of a coined brand name for the purpose of comparing the product without actually naming an actual competitor. ('Wikipedia tastes better and is less filling than the Encyclopedia Galactica.')

In the 1980s, during what has been referred to as the cola wars, soft-drink manufacturer Pepsi ran a series of advertisements where people, caught on hidden camera, in a blind taste test, chose Pepsi over rival Coca-Cola.

   a. 28-hour day
   b. 33 Strategies of War
   c. 1990 Clean Air Act
   d. Comparative advertising

9. An _____ is a private computer network that uses Internet technologies to securely share any part of an organization's information or operational systems with its employees. Sometimes the term refers only to the organization's internal website, but often it is a more extensive part of the organization's computer infrastructure and private websites are an important component and focal point of internal communication and collaboration.

An _____ is built from the same concepts and technologies used for the Internet, such as client-server computing and the Internet Protocol Suite (TCP/IP.)

   a. Intranet
   b. A Stake in the Outcome
   c. A4e
   d. AAAI

10. An _____ is a private network that uses Internet protocols, network connectivity, and possibly the public telecommunication system to securely share part of an organization's information or operations with suppliers, vendors, partners, customers or other businesses. An _____ can be viewed as part of a company's intranet that is extended to users outside the company (e.g.: normally over the Internet.) It has also been described as a 'state of mind' in which the Internet is perceived as a way to do business with a preapproved set of other companies business-to-business (B2B), in isolation from all other Internet users.
   a. A Stake in the Outcome
   b. AAAI
   c. A4e
   d. Extranet

11. _____ are companies whose headcount or turnover falls below certain limits.

Chapter 1. Introduction to e-business and e-commerce 5

These types of enterprises occur commonly in the European Union and in international organizations, such as the World Bank, the United Nations and the WTO. The term small and medium-sized businesses or SMBs is predominantly used in the USA.

a. Small and medium enterprises
b. Prospero Business Suite
c. Compensation methods
d. Command center

12. In economics, business, retail, and accounting, a _____ is the value of money that has been used up to produce something, and hence is not available for use anymore. In economics, a _____ is an alternative that is given up as a result of a decision. In business, the _____ may be one of acquisition, in which case the amount of money expended to acquire it is counted as _____.

a. Fixed costs
b. Cost allocation
c. Cost overrun
d. Cost

13. _____ is the state or fact of exclusive rights and control over property, which may be an object, land/real estate or intellectual property. An _____ right is also referred to as title. The concept of _____ has existed for thousands of years and in all cultures.

a. A4e
b. A Stake in the Outcome
c. Emanation of the state
d. Ownership

14. In economics, and cost accounting, _____ describes the total economic cost of production and is made up of variable costs, which vary according to the quantity of a good produced and include inputs such as labor and raw materials, plus fixed costs, which are independent of the quantity of a good produced and include inputs (capital) that cannot be varied in the short term, such as buildings and machinery. _____ in economics includes the total opportunity cost of each factor of production in addition to fixed and variable costs.

The rate at which _____ changes as the amount produced changes is called marginal cost.

a. 28-hour day
b. 1990 Clean Air Act
c. 33 Strategies of War
d. Total cost

15. _____ is a financial estimate designed to help consumers and enterprise managers assess direct and indirect costs It is a form of full cost accounting.
a. 28-hour day
b. 1990 Clean Air Act
c. 33 Strategies of War
d. Total cost of ownership

16. _____ is a strategic planning method used to evaluate the Strengths, Weaknesses, Opportunities, and Threats involved in a project or in a business venture. It involves specifying the objective of the business venture or project and identifying the internal and external factors that are favorable and unfavorable to achieving that objective. The technique is credited to Albert Humphrey, who led a convention at Stanford University in the 1960s and 1970s using data from Fortune 500 companies.
a. Corporate image
b. Marketing
c. SWOT analysis
d. Market share

Chapter 2. E-commerce fundamentals

1. _____, commonly known as e-commerce, consists of the buying and selling of products or services over electronic systems such as the Internet and other computer networks. The amount of trade conducted electronically has grown extraordinarily with widespread Internet usage. The use of commerce is conducted in this way, spurring and drawing on innovations in electronic funds transfer, supply chain management, Internet marketing, online transaction processing, electronic data interchange (EDI), inventory management systems, and automated data collection systems.

   a. Online shopping
   b. A Stake in the Outcome
   c. Electronic Commerce
   d. A4e

2. _____ comprises a range of practices used in an organisation to identify, create, represent, distribute and enable adoption of insights and experiences. Such insights and experiences comprise knowledge, either embodied in individuals or embedded in organisational processes or practice.

   An established discipline since 1991 , _____ includes courses taught in the fields of business administration, information systems, management, and library and information sciences .

   a. 28-hour day
   b. 1990 Clean Air Act
   c. 33 Strategies of War
   d. Knowledge management

3. _____ describes commerce transactions between businesses, such as between a manufacturer and a wholesaler, or between a wholesaler and a retailer. Contrasting terms are business-to-consumer (B2C) and business-to-government (B2G.)

   The volume of B2B transactions is much higher than the volume of B2C transactions.

   a. Business-to-business
   b. Product bundling
   c. Category management
   d. Market environment

4. Business-to-consumer describes activities of businesses serving end consumers with products and/or services.

   An example of a _____ transaction would be a person buying a pair of shoes from a retailer. The transactions that led to the shoes being available for purchase, that is the purchase of the leather, laces, rubber, etc.

a. B2C
b. Green marketing
c. PEST analysis
d. Market environment

5. In economics, _____ is the removal of intermediaries in a supply chain: 'cutting out the middleman'. Instead of going through traditional distribution channels, which had some type of intermediate (such as a distributor, wholesaler, broker, or agent), companies may now deal with every customer directly, for example via the Internet. One important factor is a drop in the cost of servicing customers directly.

a. Disintermediation
b. 1990 Clean Air Act
c. Virtual enterprise
d. 28-hour day

6. _____ is one of the four elements of marketing mix. An organization or set of organizations (go-betweens) involved in the process of making a product or service available for use or consumption by a consumer or business user.

The other three parts of the marketing mix are product, pricing, and promotion.

a. Distribution
b. Missing completely at random
c. Job creation programs
d. Matching theory

7. _____ is an integrated communications-based process through which individuals and communities discover that existing and newly-identified needs and wants may be satisfied by the products and services of others.

_____ is defined by the American _____ Association as the activity, set of institutions, and processes for creating, communicating, delivering, and exchanging offerings that have value for customers, clients, partners, and society at large. The term developed from the original meaning which referred literally to going to market, as in shopping, or going to a market to buy or sell goods or services.

a. Customer relationship management
b. Marketing
c. Market development
d. Disruptive technology

Chapter 2. E-commerce fundamentals

8. A _____ is a process that can allow an organization to concentrate its limited resources on the greatest opportunities to increase sales and achieve a sustainable competitive advantage. A _____ should be centered around the key concept that customer satisfaction is the main goal.

A _____ is a written plan which combines product development, promotion, distribution, and pricing approach, identifies the firm's marketing goals, and explains how they will be achieved within a stated timeframe.

   a. Product bundling
   b. Marketing strategy
   c. Category management
   d. Disruptive technology

9. _____ of the learning curve effect and the closely related experience curve effect express the relationship between equations for experience and efficiency or between efficiency gains and investment in the effort. The experience of 'learning curves' was first observed by the 19th Century German psychologist Hermann Ebbinghaus according to the difficulty of memorizing varying numbers of verbal stimuli, and subsequent learning about the complex processes of learning are discussed in the

.

The rule used for representing the learning curve effect states that the more times a task has been performed, the less time will be required on each subsequent iteration.

   a. Models
   b. Distribution
   c. Point biserial correlation coefficient
   d. Spatial Decision Support Systems

10.

_____ is a systematic method to improve the 'value' of goods or products and services by using an examination of function. Value, as defined, is the ratio of function to cost. Value can therefore be increased by either improving the function or reducing the cost.

   a. Value engineering
   b. Capacity planning
   c. Cellular manufacturing
   d. Master production schedule

11. _____ is a form of communication that typically attempts to persuade potential customers to purchase or to consume more of a particular brand of product or service. 'While now central to the contemporary global economy and the reproduction of global production networks, it is only quite recently that _____ has been more than a marginal influence on patterns of sales and production. The formation of modern _____ was intimately bound up with the emergence of new forms of monopoly capitalism around the end of the 19th and beginning of the 20th century as one element in corporate strategies to create, organize and where possible control markets, especially for mass produced consumer goods.
   a. A Stake in the Outcome
   b. Advertising
   c. AAAI
   d. A4e

12. _____ is a type of advertising that typically contains text (i.e., copy), logos, photographs or other images, location maps, and similar items. In periodicals, _____ can appear on the same page as, or on the page adjacent to, general editorial content. In contrast, classified advertising generally appears in a distinct section, was traditionally text-only, and was available in a limited selection of typefaces.
   a. 28-hour day
   b. 1990 Clean Air Act
   c. 33 Strategies of War
   d. Display advertising

13. In law, _____ is the term to describe a partnership between two or more parties.

In England a number of statutes on the subject have been passed, the chief being the Bastardy Act of 1845, and the Bastardy Laws Amendment Acts of 1872 and 1873. The mother of a bastard may summon the putative father to petty sessions within twelve months of the birth (or at any later time if he is proved to have contributed to the child's support within twelve months after the birth), and the justices, as after hearing evidence on both sides, may, if the mother's evidence be corroborated in some material particular, adjudge the man to be the putative father of the child, and order him to pay a sum not exceeding five shillings a week for its maintenance, together with a sum for expenses incidental to the birth, or the funeral expenses, if it has died before the date of order, and the costs of the proceedings.

   a. Abraham Harold Maslow
   b. Adam Smith
   c. Affiliation
   d. Affiliation

14. A _____ is a framework for creating economic, social, and/or other forms of value. The term _____ is thus used for a broad range of informal and formal descriptions to represent core aspects of a business, including purpose, offerings, strategies, infrastructure, organizational structures, trading practices, and operational processes and policies.

Conceptualizations of _____s try to formalize informal descriptions into building blocks and their relationships.

a. Gap analysis
b. Business networking
c. Business model
d. Business model design

15. The phrase mergers and _____s refers to the aspect of corporate strategy, corporate finance and management dealing with the buying, selling and combining of different companies that can aid, finance, or help a growing company in a given industry grow rapidly without having to create another business entity.

An _____, also known as a takeover or a buyout, is the buying of one company (the 'target') by another. An _____ may be friendly or hostile.

a. A4e
b. AAAI
c. A Stake in the Outcome
d. Acquisition

16. In economics, business, retail, and accounting, a _____ is the value of money that has been used up to produce something, and hence is not available for use anymore. In economics, a _____ is an alternative that is given up as a result of a decision. In business, the _____ may be one of acquisition, in which case the amount of money expended to acquire it is counted as _____.

a. Fixed costs
b. Cost allocation
c. Cost
d. Cost overrun

17. _____, commonly referred to as 'eBusiness' or 'e-Business', may be defined as the utilization of information and communication technologies (ICT) in support of all the activities of business. Commerce constitutes the exchange of products and services between businesses, groups and individuals and hence can be seen as one of the essential activities of any business. Hence, electronic commerce or eCommerce focuses on the use of ICT to enable the external activities and relationships of the business with individuals, groups and other businesses.

a. A Stake in the Outcome
b. AAAI
c. A4e
d. Electronic business

Chapter 3. E-business infrastructure

1. _____, commonly referred to as 'eBusiness' or 'e-Business', may be defined as the utilization of information and communication technologies (ICT) in support of all the activities of business. Commerce constitutes the exchange of products and services between businesses, groups and individuals and hence can be seen as one of the essential activities of any business. Hence, electronic commerce or eCommerce focuses on the use of ICT to enable the external activities and relationships of the business with individuals, groups and other businesses .
    a. A Stake in the Outcome
    b. A4e
    c. AAAI
    d. Electronic business

2. _____ refers to the practice of making websites usable by people of all abilities and disabilities. When sites are correctly designed, developed and edited, all users can have equal access to information and functionality. For example, when a site is coded with semantically meaningful HTML, with textual equivalents provided for images and with links named meaningfully, this helps blind users using text-to-speech software and/or text-to-Braille hardware.
    a. 1990 Clean Air Act
    b. 28-hour day
    c. Web accessibility
    d. 33 Strategies of War

3. An _____ is a private computer network that uses Internet technologies to securely share any part of an organization's information or operational systems with its employees. Sometimes the term refers only to the organization's internal website, but often it is a more extensive part of the organization's computer infrastructure and private websites are an important component and focal point of internal communication and collaboration.

    An _____ is built from the same concepts and technologies used for the Internet, such as client-server computing and the Internet Protocol Suite (TCP/IP.)

    a. Intranet
    b. AAAI
    c. A Stake in the Outcome
    d. A4e

4. An _____ is a private network that uses Internet protocols, network connectivity, and possibly the public telecommunication system to securely share part of an organization's information or operations with suppliers, vendors, partners, customers or other businesses. An _____ can be viewed as part of a company's intranet that is extended to users outside the company (e.g.: normally over the Internet.) It has also been described as a 'state of mind' in which the Internet is perceived as a way to do business with a preapproved set of other companies business-to-business (B2B), in isolation from all other Internet users.

a. A4e
b. A Stake in the Outcome
c. AAAI
d. Extranet

5. In economics, business, retail, and accounting, a _____ is the value of money that has been used up to produce something, and hence is not available for use anymore. In economics, a _____ is an alternative that is given up as a result of a decision. In business, the _____ may be one of acquisition, in which case the amount of money expended to acquire it is counted as _____.

a. Fixed costs
b. Cost overrun
c. Cost allocation
d. Cost

6. _____ is the state or fact of exclusive rights and control over property, which may be an object, land/real estate or intellectual property. An _____ right is also referred to as title. The concept of _____ has existed for thousands of years and in all cultures.

a. Emanation of the state
b. A4e
c. A Stake in the Outcome
d. Ownership

7. In economics, and cost accounting, _____ describes the total economic cost of production and is made up of variable costs, which vary according to the quantity of a good produced and include inputs such as labor and raw materials, plus fixed costs, which are independent of the quantity of a good produced and include inputs (capital) that cannot be varied in the short term, such as buildings and machinery. _____ in economics includes the total opportunity cost of each factor of production in addition to fixed and variable costs.

The rate at which _____ changes as the amount produced changes is called marginal cost.

a. 28-hour day
b. 1990 Clean Air Act
c. 33 Strategies of War
d. Total cost

8. _____ is a financial estimate designed to help consumers and enterprise managers assess direct and indirect costs It is a form of full cost accounting.

a. 28-hour day
b. Total cost of ownership
c. 1990 Clean Air Act
d. 33 Strategies of War

9. A _____ is a graphic representation of the maturity, adoption and business application of specific technologies. The term was coined by Gartner, an analyst/research house, based in the United States, that provides opinions, advice and data on the global information technology industry.

Since 1995, Gartner has used _____s to characterize the over-enthusiasm or 'hype' and subsequent disappointment that typically happens with the introduction of new technologies.

a. 1990 Clean Air Act
b. 33 Strategies of War
c. 28-hour day
d. Hype cycle

10. The _____ is an abstract description for layered communications and computer network protocol design. It was developed as part of the Open Systems Interconnection (OSI) initiative. In its most basic form, it divides network architecture into seven layers which, from top to bottom, are the Application, Presentation, Session, Transport, Network, Data-Link, and Physical Layers.
a. A Stake in the Outcome
b. AAAI
c. A4e
d. Open Systems Interconnection Reference Model

11. _____ is a strategic planning method used to evaluate the Strengths, Weaknesses, Opportunities, and Threats involved in a project or in a business venture. It involves specifying the objective of the business venture or project and identifying the internal and external factors that are favorable and unfavorable to achieving that objective. The technique is credited to Albert Humphrey, who led a convention at Stanford University in the 1960s and 1970s using data from Fortune 500 companies.
a. Marketing
b. Corporate image
c. SWOT analysis
d. Market share

Chapter 3. E-business infrastructure

12. _____ is multimedia that is constantly received by, and normally presented to, an end-user while it is being delivered by a streaming provider (the term 'presented' is used in this article in a general sense that includes audio or video playback.) The name refers to the delivery method of the medium rather than to the medium itself. The distinction is usually applied to media that are distributed over telecommunications networks, as most other delivery systems are either inherently streaming (e.g. radio, television) or inherently non-streaming (e.g. books, video cassettes, audio CDs.)
    a. 1990 Clean Air Act
    b. 28-hour day
    c. Streaming media
    d. 33 Strategies of War

13. _____ is, in very basic words, a position a firm occupies against its competitors.

According to Michael Porter, the three methods for creating a sustainable _____ are through:

1. Cost leadership

2. Differentiation

3. Focus (economics)

    a. Theory Z
    b. 28-hour day
    c. 1990 Clean Air Act
    d. Competitive advantage

14. _____ is an advertisement in which a particular product specifically mentions a competitor by name for the express purpose of showing why the competitor is inferior to the product naming it.

This should not be confused with parody advertisements, where a fictional product is being advertised for the purpose of poking fun at the particular advertisement, nor should it be confused with the use of a coined brand name for the purpose of comparing the product without actually naming an actual competitor. ('Wikipedia tastes better and is less filling than the Encyclopedia Galactica.')

In the 1980s, during what has been referred to as the cola wars, soft-drink manufacturer Pepsi ran a series of advertisements where people, caught on hidden camera, in a blind taste test, chose Pepsi over rival Coca-Cola.

a. 1990 Clean Air Act
b. 28-hour day
c. 33 Strategies of War
d. Comparative advertising

15. A _____ is a list of the general tasks and responsibilities of a position. Typically, it also includes to whom the position reports, specifications such as the qualifications needed by the person in the job, salary range for the position, etc. A _____ is usually developed by conducting a job analysis, which includes examining the tasks and sequences of tasks necessary to perform the job.
   a. Job description
   b. Recruitment advertising
   c. Recruitment
   d. Recruitment Process Insourcing

16. _____ measures the performance of a system. Certain goals are defined and the _____ gives the percentage to which they should be achieved.

Examples

- Percentage of calls answered in a call center.
- Percentage of customers waiting less than a given fixed time.
- Percentage of customers that do not experience a stock out.

_____ is used in supply chain management and in inventory management to measure the performance of inventory systems.

Under stochastic conditions it is unavoidable that in some periods the inventory on hand is not sufficient to deliver the complete demand and, as a consequence, that part of the demand is filled only after an inventory-related waiting time.

   a. 33 Strategies of War
   b. 1990 Clean Air Act
   c. Service level
   d. 28-hour day

17. _____ is a company-wide computer software system used to manage and coordinate all the resources, information, and functions of a business from shared data stores.

An _____ system has a service-oriented architecture with modular hardware and software units and 'services' that communicate on a local area network. The modular design allows a business to add or reconfigure modules (perhaps from different vendors) while preserving data integrity in one shared database that may be centralized or distributed.

   a. A4e
   b. Enterprise resource planning
   c. AAAI
   d. A Stake in the Outcome

18. In economics, _____ is a measure of the relative satisfaction from consumption of various goods and services. Given this measure, one may speak meaningfully of increasing or decreasing _____, and thereby explain economic behavior in terms of attempts to increase one's _____. For illustrative purposes, changes in _____ are sometimes expressed in units called utils.
   a. Indirect utility function
   b. A Stake in the Outcome
   c. Ordinal utility
   d. Utility

19. _____ is the ability to conduct commerce, using a mobile device e.g. a mobile phone, a PDA, a smartphone and other emerging mobile equipment such as dashtop mobile devices. _____ has been defined as follows:

'_____ is any transaction, involving the transfer of ownership or rights to use goods and services, which is initiated and/or completed by using mobile access to computer-mediated networks with the help of an electronic device.'

_____ was born in 1997 when the first two mobile phone enabled Coca Cola vending machines were installed the Helsinki area in Finland. They used SMS text messages to send the payment to the vending machines.

   a. Adam Smith
   b. Mobile commerce
   c. Abraham Harold Maslow
   d. Affiliation

Chapter 4. E-environment

1. _____ is a process of gathering, analyzing, and dispensing information for tactical or strategic purposes. The _____ process entails obtaining both factual and subjective information on the business environments in which a company is operating or considering entering.

There are three ways of scanning the business environment:

- Ad-hoc scanning - Short term, infrequent examinations usually initiated by a crisis
- Regular scanning - Studies done on a regular schedule (say, once a year)
- Continuous scanning(also called continuous learning) - continuous structured data collection and processing on a broad range of environmental factors

Most commentators feel that in today's turbulent business environment the best scanning method available is continuous scanning. This allows the firm to :

-act quickly-take advantage of opportunities before competitors do-respond to environmental threats before significant damage is done

   a. A Stake in the Outcome
   b. AAAI
   c. A4e
   d. Environmental scanning

2. In economics, _____ is the desire to own something and the ability to pay for it. The term _____ signifies the ability or the willingness to buy a particular commodity at a given point of time.
   a. 33 Strategies of War
   b. 1990 Clean Air Act
   c. 28-hour day
   d. Demand

3. _____ or _____ data refers to selected population characteristics as used in government, marketing or opinion research, or the _____ profiles used in such research. Note the distinction from the term 'demography' Commonly-used _____s include race, age, income, disabilities, mobility (in terms of travel time to work or number of vehicles available), educational attainment, home ownership, employment status, and even location.
   a. Demographic
   b. Affiliation
   c. Adam Smith
   d. Abraham Harold Maslow

Chapter 4. E-environment

4. _____, commonly referred to as 'eBusiness' or 'e-Business', may be defined as the utilization of information and communication technologies (ICT) in support of all the activities of business. Commerce constitutes the exchange of products and services between businesses, groups and individuals and hence can be seen as one of the essential activities of any business. Hence, electronic commerce or eCommerce focuses on the use of ICT to enable the external activities and relationships of the business with individuals, groups and other businesses.

   a. AAAI
   b. A Stake in the Outcome
   c. A4e
   d. Electronic business

5. _____, commonly known as e-commerce, consists of the buying and selling of products or services over electronic systems such as the Internet and other computer networks. The amount of trade conducted electronically has grown extraordinarily with widespread Internet usage. The use of commerce is conducted in this way, spurring and drawing on innovations in electronic funds transfer, supply chain management, Internet marketing, online transaction processing, electronic data interchange (EDI), inventory management systems, and automated data collection systems.

   a. A4e
   b. Electronic Commerce
   c. Online shopping
   d. A Stake in the Outcome

6.

_____ is a systematic method to improve the 'value' of goods or products and services by using an examination of function. Value, as defined, is the ratio of function to cost. Value can therefore be increased by either improving the function or reducing the cost.

   a. Cellular manufacturing
   b. Master production schedule
   c. Capacity planning
   d. Value engineering

7. _____ is an advertisement in which a particular product specifically mentions a competitor by name for the express purpose of showing why the competitor is inferior to the product naming it.

This should not be confused with parody advertisements, where a fictional product is being advertised for the purpose of poking fun at the particular advertisement, nor should it be confused with the use of a coined brand name for the purpose of comparing the product without actually naming an actual competitor. ('Wikipedia tastes better and is less filling than the Encyclopedia Galactica.')

Chapter 4. E-environment

In the 1980s, during what has been referred to as the cola wars, soft-drink manufacturer Pepsi ran a series of advertisements where people, caught on hidden camera, in a blind taste test, chose Pepsi over rival Coca-Cola.

a. 1990 Clean Air Act
b. 28-hour day
c. 33 Strategies of War
d. Comparative advertising

8. _____ is an integrated communications-based process through which individuals and communities discover that existing and newly-identified needs and wants may be satisfied by the products and services of others.

_____ is defined by the American _____ Association as the activity, set of institutions, and processes for creating, communicating, delivering, and exchanging offerings that have value for customers, clients, partners, and society at large. The term developed from the original meaning which referred literally to going to market, as in shopping, or going to a market to buy or sell goods or services.

a. Disruptive technology
b. Customer relationship management
c. Market development
d. Marketing

9. The buzzwords _____ and viral advertising refer to marketing techniques that use pre-existing social networks to produce increases in brand awareness or to achieve other marketing objectives (such as product sales) through self-replicating viral processes, analogous to the spread of pathological and computer viruses. It can be word-of-mouth delivered or enhanced by the network effects of the Internet. Viral promotions may take the form of video clips, interactive Flash games, advergames, ebooks, brandable software, images, or even text messages.
a. 33 Strategies of War
b. Viral marketing
c. 1990 Clean Air Act
d. 28-hour day

10. The general definition of an _____ is an evaluation of a person, organization, system, process, project or product. _____s are performed to ascertain the validity and reliability of information; also to provide an assessment of a system's internal control. The goal of an _____ is to express an opinion on the person / organization/system (etc) in question, under evaluation based on work done on a test basis.

a. Audit
b. A Stake in the Outcome
c. Audit committee
d. Internal control

11. A _____ is a distinctive sign or indicator used by an individual, business organization, or other legal entity to identify that the products and/or services to consumers with which the _____ appears originate from a unique source and to distinguish its products or services from those of other entities.

a. Virtual team
b. Kanban
c. Trademark
d. Succession planning

12. _____ is a form of communication that typically attempts to persuade potential customers to purchase or to consume more of a particular brand of product or service. 'While now central to the contemporary global economy and the reproduction of global production networks, it is only quite recently that _____ has been more than a marginal influence on patterns of sales and production. The formation of modern _____ was intimately bound up with the emergence of new forms of monopoly capitalism around the end of the 19th and beginning of the 20th century as one element in corporate strategies to create, organize and where possible control markets, especially for mass produced consumer goods.

a. A4e
b. A Stake in the Outcome
c. AAAI
d. Advertising

13. _____ are legal property rights over creations of the mind, both artistic and commercial, and the corresponding fields of law. Under _____ law, owners are granted certain exclusive rights to a variety of intangible assets, such as musical, literary, and artistic works; ideas, discoveries and inventions; and words, phrases, symbols, and designs. Common types of _____ include copyrights, trademarks, patents, industrial design rights and trade secrets.

a. Intent
b. Intellectual property
c. Equal Pay Act
d. Unemployment Action Center

14. _____ plant, and equipment, is a term used in accountancy for assets and property which cannot easily be converted into cash. This can be compared with current assets such as cash or bank accounts, which are described as liquid assets. In most cases, only tangible assets are referred to as fixed.

a. 1990 Clean Air Act
b. 33 Strategies of War
c. 28-hour day
d. Fixed asset

15. In decision theory and estimation theory, the _____ of an estimator, $\hat{\theta}$, of an unknown parameter of the distribution, θ, is the expected value of the loss function

$$R(\theta, \hat{\theta}) = \mathbb{E}_\theta L(\theta, \hat{\theta}) = \int L(\theta, \hat{\theta})\, dP_\theta.$$

where dP_θ is a probability measure parametrized by θ.

- For a scalar parameter θ and a quadratic loss function,

$$L(\theta, \hat{\theta}) = (\theta - \hat{\theta})^2$$

  the _____ function becomes the mean squared error of the estimate,

$$R(\theta, \hat{\theta}) = E_\theta(\theta - \hat{\theta})^2$$

- In density estimation, the unknown parameter is probability density itself. The loss function is typically chosen to be a norm in an appropriate function space. For example, for L^2 norm,

$$L(f, \hat{f}) = \|f - \hat{f}\|_2^2$$

  the _____ function becomes the mean integrated squared error

$$R(f, \hat{f}) = E\|f - \hat{f}\|^2$$

a. Risk
b. Linear model
c. Financial modeling
d. Risk aversion

Chapter 4. E-environment

16. _____ is a strategic planning method used to evaluate the Strengths, Weaknesses, Opportunities, and Threats involved in a project or in a business venture. It involves specifying the objective of the business venture or project and identifying the internal and external factors that are favorable and unfavorable to achieving that objective. The technique is credited to Albert Humphrey, who led a convention at Stanford University in the 1960s and 1970s using data from Fortune 500 companies.

   a. Corporate image
   b. SWOT analysis
   c. Marketing
   d. Market share

17. _____ is exchange of capital, goods, and services across international borders or territories. In most countries, it represents a significant share of gross domestic product (GDP.) While _____ has been present throughout much of history, its economic, social, and political importance has been on the rise in recent centuries.

   a. International trade
   b. A4e
   c. A Stake in the Outcome
   d. AAAI

18. _____ in its literal sense is the process of transformation of local or regional phenomena into global ones. It can be described as a process by which the people of the world are unified into a single society and function together.

   This process is a combination of economic, technological, sociocultural and political forces.

   a. Cost Management
   b. Collaborative Planning, Forecasting and Replenishment
   c. Histogram
   d. Globalization

19. _____ is a broad label that refers to any individuals or households that use goods and services generated within the economy. The concept of a _____ is used in different contexts, so that the usage and significance of the term may vary.

   Typically when business people and economists talk of _____s they are talking about person as _____, an aggregated commodity item with little individuality other than that expressed in the buy/not-buy decision.

a. 1990 Clean Air Act
b. 28-hour day
c. Consumer
d. 33 Strategies of War

20. _____ are companies whose headcount or turnover falls below certain limits.

These types of enterprises occur commonly in the European Union and in international organizations, such as the World Bank, the United Nations and the WTO. The term small and medium-sized businesses or SMBs is predominantly used in the USA.

a. Command center
b. Prospero Business Suite
c. Compensation methods
d. Small and medium enterprises

21. _____ is the process by which a new idea or new product is accepted by the market. The rate of _____ is the speed that the new idea spreads from one consumer to the next. Adoption is similar to _____ except that it deals with the psychological processes an individual goes through, rather than an aggregate market process.

a. Mass marketing
b. Value chain
c. Category management
d. Diffusion

22. A _____ is a graphic representation of the maturity, adoption and business application of specific technologies. The term was coined by Gartner, an analyst/research house, based in the United States, that provides opinions, advice and data on the global information technology industry.

Since 1995, Gartner has used _____s to characterize the over-enthusiasm or 'hype' and subsequent disappointment that typically happens with the introduction of new technologies.

a. 33 Strategies of War
b. 28-hour day
c. 1990 Clean Air Act
d. Hype cycle

Chapter 5. E-business strategy

1. _____ is a strategic planning method used to evaluate the Strengths, Weaknesses, Opportunities, and Threats involved in a project or in a business venture. It involves specifying the objective of the business venture or project and identifying the internal and external factors that are favorable and unfavorable to achieving that objective. The technique is credited to Albert Humphrey, who led a convention at Stanford University in the 1960s and 1970s using data from Fortune 500 companies.
   a. Corporate image
   b. SWOT analysis
   c. Marketing
   d. Market share

2. _____ is an advertisement in which a particular product specifically mentions a competitor by name for the express purpose of showing why the competitor is inferior to the product naming it.

   This should not be confused with parody advertisements, where a fictional product is being advertised for the purpose of poking fun at the particular advertisement, nor should it be confused with the use of a coined brand name for the purpose of comparing the product without actually naming an actual competitor. ('Wikipedia tastes better and is less filling than the Encyclopedia Galactica.')

   In the 1980s, during what has been referred to as the cola wars, soft-drink manufacturer Pepsi ran a series of advertisements where people, caught on hidden camera, in a blind taste test, chose Pepsi over rival Coca-Cola.

   a. Comparative advertising
   b. 28-hour day
   c. 1990 Clean Air Act
   d. 33 Strategies of War

3. _____ of the learning curve effect and the closely related experience curve effect express the relationship between equations for experience and efficiency or between efficiency gains and investment in the effort. The experience of 'learning curves' was first observed by the 19th Century German psychologist Hermann Ebbinghaus according to the difficulty of memorizing varying numbers of verbal stimuli, and subsequent learning about the complex processes of learning are discussed in the

   The rule used for representing the learning curve effect states that the more times a task has been performed, the less time will be required on each subsequent iteration.

   a. Distribution
   b. Spatial Decision Support Systems
   c. Point biserial correlation coefficient
   d. Models

Chapter 5. E-business strategy

4. The term _____ is used in various contexts. For example, in business process modeling the enterprise _____ is often referred to as the business _____. Process models are core concepts in the discipline of Process Engineering.
   a. 1990 Clean Air Act
   b. 28-hour day
   c. Process model
   d. 33 Strategies of War

5. _____, commonly referred to as 'eBusiness' or 'e-Business', may be defined as the utilization of information and communication technologies (ICT) in support of all the activities of business. Commerce constitutes the exchange of products and services between businesses, groups and individuals and hence can be seen as one of the essential activities of any business. Hence, electronic commerce or eCommerce focuses on the use of ICT to enable the external activities and relationships of the business with individuals, groups and other businesses.
   a. Electronic business
   b. A Stake in the Outcome
   c. A4e
   d. AAAI

6. _____ is an increasingly broadening term with which an organization, or other human system describes the combination of traditionally administrative personnel functions with acquisition and application of skills, knowledge and experience, Employee Relations and resource planning at various levels. The field draws upon concepts developed in Industrial/Organizational Psychology and System Theory. _____ has at least two related interpretations depending on context. The original usage derives from political economy and economics, where it was traditionally called labor, one of four factors of production although this perspective is changing as a function of new and ongoing research into more strategic approaches at national levels. This first usage is used more in terms of '_____ development', and can go beyond just organizations to the level of nations. The more traditional usage within corporations and businesses refers to the individuals within a firm or agency, and to the portion of the organization that deals with hiring, firing, training, and other personnel issues, typically referred to as `_____ management'.
   a. Human resources
   b. Bradford Factor
   c. Human resource management
   d. Progressive discipline

7. In economics, _____ is the desire to own something and the ability to pay for it. The term _____ signifies the ability or the willingness to buy a particular commodity at a given point of time.

a. 33 Strategies of War
b. 28-hour day
c. 1990 Clean Air Act
d. Demand

8. _____ in marketing and strategic management is an assessment of the strengths and weaknesses of current and potential competitors. This analysis provides both an offensive and defensive strategic context through which to identify opportunities and threats. Competitor profiling coalesces all of the relevant sources of _____ into one framework in the support of efficient and effective strategy formulation, implementation, monitoring and adjustment.

a. Competitor or Competitive Intelligence
b. 28-hour day
c. Competitor analysis
d. 1990 Clean Air Act

9. _____ is something that a firm can do well and that meets the following three conditions:

Competencies are things that companys execute well across several business units or product sectors.

Firms usually have few competencies, but these are usually less liable to change rapidly.

1. It provides consumer benefits
2. It is not easy for competitors to imitate
3. It can be leveraged widely to many products and markets.

A _____ can take various forms, including technical/subject matter know-how, a reliable process and/or close relationships with customers and suppliers (Mascarenhas et al. 1998.)

a. NAIRU
b. Dominant Design
c. Learning-by-doing
d. Core competency

10.

_____ is a systematic method to improve the 'value' of goods or products and services by using an examination of function. Value, as defined, is the ratio of function to cost. Value can therefore be increased by either improving the function or reducing the cost.

a. Capacity planning
b. Value engineering
c. Cellular manufacturing
d. Master production schedule

11. In management, _____ is an informal term that includes all forms of value that determine the health and well-being of the firm in the long-run. _____ expands concept of value of the firm beyond economic value (also known as economic profit, Economic value added, and Shareholder value) to include other forms of value such as employee value, customer value, supplier value, channel partner value, alliance partner value, managerial value, and societal value. Many of these forms of value are not directly measured in monetary terms.
   a. Catfish effect
   b. Real Property Administrator
   c. Frenemy
   d. Business value

12. In economics, business, retail, and accounting, a _____ is the value of money that has been used up to produce something, and hence is not available for use anymore. In economics, a _____ is an alternative that is given up as a result of a decision. In business, the _____ may be one of acquisition, in which case the amount of money expended to acquire it is counted as _____.
   a. Cost overrun
   b. Cost allocation
   c. Fixed costs
   d. Cost

13. In decision theory and estimation theory, the _____ of an estimator, $\hat{\theta}$, of an unknown parameter of the distribution, θ, is the expected value of the loss function

$$R(\theta, \hat{\theta}) = \mathbb{E}_\theta L(\theta, \hat{\theta}) = \int L(\theta, \hat{\theta}) \, dP_\theta.$$

where dP_θ is a probability measure parametrized by θ.

- For a scalar parameter θ and a quadratic loss function,

$$L(\theta, \hat{\theta}) = (\theta - \hat{\theta})^2$$

the _____ function becomes the mean squared error of the estimate,

$$R(\theta, \hat{\theta}) = E_\theta(\theta - \hat{\theta})^2$$

- In density estimation, the unknown parameter is probability density itself. The loss function is typically chosen to be a norm in an appropriate function space. For example, for L^2 norm,

$$L(f, \hat{f}) = \|f - \hat{f}\|_2^2$$

the _____ function becomes the mean integrated squared error

$$R(f, \hat{f}) = E\|f - \hat{f}\|^2$$

a. Risk
b. Financial modeling
c. Linear model
d. Risk aversion

14. _____ is the identification, assessment, and prioritization of risks followed by coordinated and economical application of resources to minimize, monitor, and control the probability and/or impact of unfortunate events.. Risks can come from uncertainty in financial markets, project failures, legal liabilities, credit risk, accidents, natural causes and disasters as well as deliberate attacks from an adversary. Several _____ standards have been developed including the Project Management Institute, the National Institute of Science and Technology, actuarial societies, and ISO standards.
   a. Succession planning
   b. Trademark
   c. Risk management
   d. Kanban

Chapter 5. E-business strategy

15. _____ is a forward looking process for setting goals and regularly checking progress toward achieving those goals. It is a continual feedback process whereby the actual outputs are measured and compared with the desired goals. Any discrepancy or gap is then fed back into changing the inputs of the process, so as to achieve the desired goals or outputs.

a. Performance management
b. 1990 Clean Air Act
c. 33 Strategies of War
d. 28-hour day

16. _____ is the process whereby an organization establishes the parameters within which programs, investments, and acquisitions are reaching the desired results. Performance Reference Model of the Federal Enterprise Architecture, 2005.

This process of measuring performance often requires the use of statistical evidence to determine progress toward specific defined organizational objectives.

There are many types of measurements.

a. Workflow
b. Performance measurement
c. Crisis management
d. CIFMS

17. The _____ is a performance management tool for measuring whether the smaller-scale operational activities of a company are aligned with its larger-scale objectives in terms of vision and strategy.

By focusing not only on financial outcomes but also on the operational, marketing and developmental inputs to these, the _____ helps provide a more comprehensive view of a business, which in turn helps organizations act in their best long-term interests. This tool is also being used to address business response to climate change and greenhouse gas emissions.

a. Management development
b. Commercial management
c. Middle management
d. Balanced scorecard

Chapter 5. E-business strategy

18. _____ refers to the movement of cash into or out of a business or financial product. It is usually measured during a specified, finite period of time. Measurement of _____ can be used

- to determine a project's rate of return or value. The time of _____s into and out of projects are used as inputs in financial models such as internal rate of return, and net present value.
- to determine problems with a business's liquidity. Being profitable does not necessarily mean being liquid. A company can fail because of a shortage of cash, even while profitable.
- as an alternate measure of a business's profits when it is believed that accrual accounting concepts do not represent economic realities. For example, a company may be notionally profitable but generating little operational cash (as may be the case for a company that barters its products rather than selling for cash.) In such a case, the company may be deriving additional operating cash by issuing shares evaluating default risk, re-investment requirements, etc.

_____ is a generic term used differently depending on the context. It may be defined by users for their own purposes.

a. Gross profit margin
b. Cash flow
c. Gross profit
d. Sweat equity

19. _____ is the management of the flow of goods, information and other resources, including energy and people, between the point of origin and the point of consumption in order to meet the requirements of consumers (frequently, and originally, military organizations.) _____ involves the integration of information, transportation, inventory, warehousing, material-handling, and packaging, and occasionally security. _____ is a channel of the supply chain which adds the value of time and place utility.

a. 1990 Clean Air Act
b. Third-party logistics
c. 28-hour day
d. Logistics

20. _____ is the corporate management term for the act of reorganizing the legal, ownership, operational, or other structures of a company for the purpose of making it more profitable, or better organized for its present needs. Alternate reasons for _____ include a change of ownership or ownership structure, demerger repositioning debt _____ and financial _____.

a. Market value added
b. Restructuring
c. Net worth
d. Market value

Chapter 5. E-business strategy

21. A _____ is a framework for creating economic, social, and/or other forms of value. The term _____ is thus used for a broad range of informal and formal descriptions to represent core aspects of a business, including purpose, offerings, strategies, infrastructure, organizational structures, trading practices, and operational processes and policies.

Conceptualizations of _____s try to formalize informal descriptions into building blocks and their relationships.

   a. Business networking
   b. Business model
   c. Business model design
   d. Gap analysis

22. A _____ strategy targets non-buying customers in currently targeted segments. It also targets new customers in new segments. (Winer)

A marketing manager has to think about the following questions before implementing a _____ strategy: Is it profitable? Will it require the introduction of new or modified products? Is the customer and channel well enough researched and understood?

The marketing manager uses these four groups to give more focus to the market segment decision: existing customers, competitor customers, non-buying in current segments, new segments.

   a. Customer relationship management
   b. Product line
   c. Context analysis
   d. Market development

23. In business and engineering, new _____ is the term used to describe the complete process of bringing a new product or service to market. There are two parallel paths involved in the NProduct development process: one involves the idea generation, product design, and detail engineering; the other involves market research and marketing analysis. Companies typically see new _____ as the first stage in generating and commercializing new products within the overall strategic process of product life cycle management used to maintain or grow their market share.

   a. 28-hour day
   b. 1990 Clean Air Act
   c. Product development
   d. 33 Strategies of War

24. The loyalty business model is a business model used in strategic management in which company resources are employed so as to increase the loyalty of customers and other stakeholders in the expectation that corporate objectives will be met or surpassed. A typical example of this type of model is: quality of product or service leads to customer satisfaction, which leads to _____, which leads to profitability.

Fredrick Reichheld (1996) expanded the loyalty business model beyond customers and employees.

   a. Customer loyalty
   b. 1990 Clean Air Act
   c. 28-hour day
   d. 33 Strategies of War

25. _____ is an integrated communications-based process through which individuals and communities discover that existing and newly-identified needs and wants may be satisfied by the products and services of others.

_____ is defined by the American _____ Association as the activity, set of institutions, and processes for creating, communicating, delivering, and exchanging offerings that have value for customers, clients, partners, and society at large. The term developed from the original meaning which referred literally to going to market, as in shopping, or going to a market to buy or sell goods or services.

   a. Market development
   b. Disruptive technology
   c. Marketing
   d. Customer relationship management

26. In marketing, _____ has come to mean the process by which marketers try to create an image or identity in the minds of their target market for its product, brand, or organization. It is the 'relative competitive comparison' their product occupies in a given market as perceived by the target market.

Re-_____ involves changing the identity of a product, relative to the identity of competing products, in the collective minds of the target market.

   a. Context analysis
   b. Customer analytics
   c. PEST analysis
   d. Positioning

Chapter 5. E-business strategy

27. _____ is the process of comparing the cost, cycle time, productivity, or quality of a specific process or method to another that is widely considered to be an industry standard or best practice. Essentially, _____ provides a snapshot of the performance of your business and helps you understand where you are in relation to a particular standard. The result is often a business case for making changes in order to make improvements.

   a. Complementors
   b. Competitive heterogeneity
   c. Benchmarking
   d. Cost leadership

28. _____ are companies whose headcount or turnover falls below certain limits.

These types of enterprises occur commonly in the European Union and in international organizations, such as the World Bank, the United Nations and the WTO. The term small and medium-sized businesses or SMBs is predominantly used in the USA.

   a. Prospero Business Suite
   b. Command center
   c. Small and medium enterprises
   d. Compensation methods

29. An _____ is a private computer network that uses Internet technologies to securely share any part of an organization's information or operational systems with its employees. Sometimes the term refers only to the organization's internal website, but often it is a more extensive part of the organization's computer infrastructure and private websites are an important component and focal point of internal communication and collaboration.

An _____ is built from the same concepts and technologies used for the Internet, such as client-server computing and the Internet Protocol Suite (TCP/IP.)

   a. Intranet
   b. AAAI
   c. A Stake in the Outcome
   d. A4e

30. _____ is the planning process used to determine whether a firm's long term investments such as new machinery, replacement machinery, new plants, new products, and research development projects are worth pursuing. It is budget for major capital, or investment, expenditures.

Many formal methods are used in _____, including the techniques such as

- Net present value
- Profitability index
- Internal rate of return
- Modified Internal Rate of Return
- Equivalent annuity

These methods use the incremental cash flows from each potential investment, or project. Techniques based on accounting earnings and accounting rules are sometimes used - though economists consider this to be improper - such as the accounting rate of return, and 'return on investment.' Simplified and hybrid methods are used as well, such as payback period and discounted payback period.

a. Gross profit margin
b. Restricted stock
c. Capital budgeting
d. Gross profit

31. _____ refers to metrics and measures of output from production processes, per unit of input. Labor _____, for example, is typically measured as a ratio of output per labor-hour, an input. _____ may be conceived of as a metrics of the technical or engineering efficiency of production.
a. Productivity
b. Master production schedule
c. Remanufacturing
d. Value engineering

Chapter 6. Supply chain management

1. A _____ is the system of organizations, people, technology, activities, information and resources involved in moving a product or service from supplier to customer. _____ activities transform natural resources, raw materials and components into a finished product that is delivered to the end customer. In sophisticated _____ systems, used products may re-enter the _____ at any point where residual value is recyclable.
   a. Supply chain
   b. Drop shipping
   c. Wholesalers
   d. Packaging

2. _____ is the management of a network of interconnected businesses involved in the ultimate provision of product and service packages required by end customers (Harland, 1996.) _____ spans all movement and storage of raw materials, work-in-process inventory, and finished goods from point of origin to point of consumption (supply chain.)

   The definition an American professional association put forward is that _____ encompasses the planning and management of all activities involved in sourcing, procurement, conversion, and logistics management activities.

   a. Drop shipping
   b. Packaging
   c. Freight forwarder
   d. Supply chain management

3. _____ in manufacturing refers to processes that occur later on in a production sequence or production line.

   Viewing a company 'from order to cash' might have high-level processes such as Marketing, Sales, Order Entry, Manufacturing, Packaging, Shipping, Invoicing. Each of these could be deconstructed into many sub-processes and supporting processes.

   a. Genbutsu
   b. Downstream
   c. Probability-generating function
   d. Science Learning Centre

4. _____ is a broad label that refers to any individuals or households that use goods and services generated within the economy. The concept of a _____ is used in different contexts, so that the usage and significance of the term may vary.

   Typically when business people and economists talk of _____s they are talking about person as _____, an aggregated commodity item with little individuality other than that expressed in the buy/not-buy decision.

Chapter 6. Supply chain management

   a. 1990 Clean Air Act
   b. 33 Strategies of War
   c. Consumer
   d. 28-hour day

5. A _____ is one of several ways of doing research whether it is social science related or even socially related. It is an intensive study of a single group, incident, or community. Other ways include experiments, surveys, multiple histories, and analysis of archival information .

Rather than using samples and following a rigid protocol to examine limited number of variables, _____ methods involve an in-depth, longitudinal examination of a single instance or event: a case.

   a. Case study
   b. 1990 Clean Air Act
   c. Standard operating procedure
   d. Longitudinal study

6. _____ is one of the four elements of marketing mix. An organization or set of organizations (go-betweens) involved in the process of making a product or service available for use or consumption by a consumer or business user.

The other three parts of the marketing mix are product, pricing, and promotion.

   a. Job creation programs
   b. Matching theory
   c. Missing completely at random
   d. Distribution

7. _____ is an inventory strategy that strives to improve the return on investment of a business by reducing in-process inventory and its associated carrying costs. To meet _____ objectives, the process relies on signals between different points in the process. This means the process is often driven by a series of signals, or Kanban , which tell production when to make the next part. Kanban are usually 'tickets' but can be simple visual signals, such as the presence or absence of a part on a shelf. Implemented correctly, _____ can dramatically improve a manufacturing organization's return on investment, quality, and efficiency.
   a. 28-hour day
   b. Just-in-time
   c. 33 Strategies of War
   d. 1990 Clean Air Act

Chapter 6. Supply chain management

8. _____ is the management of the flow of goods, information and other resources, including energy and people, between the point of origin and the point of consumption in order to meet the requirements of consumers (frequently, and originally, military organizations.) _____ involves the integration of information, transportation, inventory, warehousing, material-handling, and packaging, and occasionally security. _____ is a channel of the supply chain which adds the value of time and place utility.
   a. 28-hour day
   b. Third-party logistics
   c. Logistics
   d. 1990 Clean Air Act

9. _____ is a strategic planning method used to evaluate the Strengths, Weaknesses, Opportunities, and Threats involved in a project or in a business venture. It involves specifying the objective of the business venture or project and identifying the internal and external factors that are favorable and unfavorable to achieving that objective. The technique is credited to Albert Humphrey, who led a convention at Stanford University in the 1960s and 1970s using data from Fortune 500 companies.
   a. SWOT analysis
   b. Corporate image
   c. Marketing
   d. Market share

10. The _____ is a concept from business management that was first described and popularized by Michael Porter in his 1985 best-seller, Competitive Advantage: Creating and Sustaining Superior Performance.

A _____ is a chain of activities. Products pass through all activities of the chain in order and at each activity the product gains some value. The chain of activities gives the products more added value than the sum of added values of all activities. It is important not to mix the concept of the _____ with the costs occurring throughout the activities.

   a. Customer relationship management
   b. Value chain
   c. Mass marketing
   d. Market development

11. _____ is the corporate management term for the act of reorganizing the legal, ownership, operational, or other structures of a company for the purpose of making it more profitable, or better organized for its present needs. Alternate reasons for _____ include a change of ownership or ownership structure, demerger repositioning debt _____ and financial _____.

Chapter 6. Supply chain management

a. Restructuring
b. Market value
c. Market value added
d. Net worth

12. The _____ is an abstract description for layered communications and computer network protocol design. It was developed as part of the Open Systems Interconnection (OSI) initiative. In its most basic form, it divides network architecture into seven layers which, from top to bottom, are the Application, Presentation, Session, Transport, Network, Data-Link, and Physical Layers.
   a. A4e
   b. AAAI
   c. A Stake in the Outcome
   d. Open Systems Interconnection Reference Model

13. In microeconomics and management, the term _____ describes a style of management control. Vertically integrated companies are united through a hierarchy with a common owner. Usually each member of the hierarchy produces a different product or (market-specific) service, and the products combine to satisfy a common need.
   a. 28-hour day
   b. 1990 Clean Air Act
   c. Vertical integration
   d. 33 Strategies of War

14. _____, commonly referred to as 'eBusiness' or 'e-Business', may be defined as the utilization of information and communication technologies (ICT) in support of all the activities of business. Commerce constitutes the exchange of products and services between businesses, groups and individuals and hence can be seen as one of the essential activities of any business. Hence, electronic commerce or eCommerce focuses on the use of ICT to enable the external activities and relationships of the business with individuals, groups and other businesses.
   a. A Stake in the Outcome
   b. AAAI
   c. Electronic business
   d. A4e

15. _____ is subcontracting a process, such as product design or manufacturing, to a third-party company. The decision to outsource is often made in the interest of lowering cost or making better use of time and energy costs, redirecting or conserving energy directed at the competencies of a particular business, or to make more efficient use of land, labor, capital, (information) technology and resources. _____ became part of the business lexicon during the 1980s.

Chapter 6. Supply chain management

a. Operant conditioning
b. Unemployment insurance
c. Outsourcing
d. Opinion leadership

16. _____ refers to the structured transmission of data between organizations by electronic means. It is used to transfer electronic documents from one computer system to another (ie) from one trading partner to another trading partner. It is more than mere E-mail; for instance, organizations might replace bills of lading and even checks with appropriate _____ messages.
   a. A Stake in the Outcome
   b. AAAI
   c. Electronic data interchange
   d. A4e

17. A _____ is a type of business entity in which partners (owners) share with each other the profits or losses of the business. _____s are often favored over corporations for taxation purposes, as the _____ structure does not generally incur a tax on profits before it is distributed to the partners (i.e. there is no dividend tax levied.) However, depending on the _____ structure and the jurisdiction in which it operates, owners of a _____ may be exposed to greater personal liability than they would as shareholders of a corporation.
   a. Federal Employers Liability Act
   b. Mediation
   c. Due process
   d. Partnership

Chapter 7. E-procurement

1. A _____ is a professional who provides advice in a particular area of expertise such as management, accountancy, the environment, entertainment, technology, law, human resources, marketing, medicine, finance, economics, public affairs, communication, engineering, sound system design, graphic design, or waste management.

   A _____ is usually an expert or a professional in a specific field and has a wide knowledge of the subject matter. A _____ usually works for a consultancy firm or is self-employed, and engages with multiple and changing clients.

   a. 28-hour day
   b. 1990 Clean Air Act
   c. 33 Strategies of War
   d. Consultant

2. In economics, business, retail, and accounting, a _____ is the value of money that has been used up to produce something, and hence is not available for use anymore. In economics, a _____ is an alternative that is given up as a result of a decision. In business, the _____ may be one of acquisition, in which case the amount of money expended to acquire it is counted as _____.

   a. Fixed costs
   b. Cost allocation
   c. Cost overrun
   d. Cost

3. In decision theory and estimation theory, the _____ of an estimator, $\hat{\theta}$, of an unknown parameter of the distribution, θ, is the expected value of the loss function

$$R(\theta, \hat{\theta}) = \mathbb{E}_\theta L(\theta, \hat{\theta}) = \int L(\theta, \hat{\theta}) \, dP_\theta.$$

where dP_θ is a probability measure parametrized by θ.

- For a scalar parameter θ and a quadratic loss function,

$$L(\theta, \hat{\theta}) = (\theta - \hat{\theta})^2$$

the _____ function becomes the mean squared error of the estimate,

$$R(\theta, \hat{\theta}) = E_\theta (\theta - \hat{\theta})^2$$

- In density estimation, the unknown parameter is probability density itself. The loss function is typically chosen to be a norm in an appropriate function space. For example, for L^2 norm,

$$L(f, \hat{f}) = \|f - \hat{f}\|_2^2$$

the _____ function becomes the mean integrated squared error

$$R(f, \hat{f}) = E\|f - \hat{f}\|^2$$

a. Linear model
b. Risk
c. Financial modeling
d. Risk aversion

4. _____ is the acquisition of goods and/or services at the best possible total cost of ownership, in the right quality and quantity, at the right time, in the right place and from the right source for the direct benefit or use of corporations, individuals generally via a contract. Simple _____ may involve nothing more than repeat purchasing. Complex _____ could involve finding long term partners - or even 'co-destiny' suppliers that might fundamentally commit one organization to another.
   a. Psychological pricing
   b. Golden parachute
   c. Procurement
   d. Sole proprietorship

Chapter 8. E-marketing

1. _____ is an integrated communications-based process through which individuals and communities discover that existing and newly-identified needs and wants may be satisfied by the products and services of others.

   _____ is defined by the American _____ Association as the activity, set of institutions, and processes for creating, communicating, delivering, and exchanging offerings that have value for customers, clients, partners, and society at large. The term developed from the original meaning which referred literally to going to market, as in shopping, or going to a market to buy or sell goods or services.

   a. Disruptive technology
   b. Market development
   c. Marketing
   d. Customer relationship management

2.

   _____ is a systematic method to improve the 'value' of goods or products and services by using an examination of function. Value, as defined, is the ratio of function to cost. Value can therefore be increased by either improving the function or reducing the cost.

   a. Master production schedule
   b. Capacity planning
   c. Value engineering
   d. Cellular manufacturing

3. _____ describes commerce transactions between businesses, such as between a manufacturer and a wholesaler, or between a wholesaler and a retailer. Contrasting terms are business-to-consumer (B2C) and business-to-government (B2G.)

   The volume of B2B transactions is much higher than the volume of B2C transactions.

   a. Business-to-business
   b. Category management
   c. Product bundling
   d. Market environment

4. _____, commonly referred to as 'eBusiness' or 'e-Business', may be defined as the utilization of information and communication technologies (ICT) in support of all the activities of business. Commerce constitutes the exchange of products and services between businesses, groups and individuals and hence can be seen as one of the essential activities of any business. Hence, electronic commerce or eCommerce focuses on the use of ICT to enable the external activities and relationships of the business with individuals, groups and other businesses .

a. A4e
b. Electronic business
c. AAAI
d. A Stake in the Outcome

5. _____, commonly known as e-commerce, consists of the buying and selling of products or services over electronic systems such as the Internet and other computer networks. The amount of trade conducted electronically has grown extraordinarily with widespread Internet usage. The use of commerce is conducted in this way, spurring and drawing on innovations in electronic funds transfer, supply chain management, Internet marketing, online transaction processing, electronic data interchange (EDI), inventory management systems, and automated data collection systems.

   a. Online shopping
   b. A Stake in the Outcome
   c. A4e
   d. Electronic Commerce

6. _____ is an advertisement in which a particular product specifically mentions a competitor by name for the express purpose of showing why the competitor is inferior to the product naming it.

This should not be confused with parody advertisements, where a fictional product is being advertised for the purpose of poking fun at the particular advertisement, nor should it be confused with the use of a coined brand name for the purpose of comparing the product without actually naming an actual competitor. ('Wikipedia tastes better and is less filling than the Encyclopedia Galactica.')

In the 1980s, during what has been referred to as the cola wars, soft-drink manufacturer Pepsi ran a series of advertisements where people, caught on hidden camera, in a blind taste test, chose Pepsi over rival Coca-Cola.

   a. 1990 Clean Air Act
   b. 28-hour day
   c. 33 Strategies of War
   d. Comparative advertising

7. _____ is a strategic planning method used to evaluate the Strengths, Weaknesses, Opportunities, and Threats involved in a project or in a business venture. It involves specifying the objective of the business venture or project and identifying the internal and external factors that are favorable and unfavorable to achieving that objective. The technique is credited to Albert Humphrey, who led a convention at Stanford University in the 1960s and 1970s using data from Fortune 500 companies.

a. Corporate image
b. Marketing
c. SWOT analysis
d. Market share

8. In economics, _____ is the desire to own something and the ability to pay for it. The term _____ signifies the ability or the willingness to buy a particular commodity at a given point of time.
   a. 28-hour day
   b. Demand
   c. 1990 Clean Air Act
   d. 33 Strategies of War

9. _____ is the process of comparing the cost, cycle time, productivity, or quality of a specific process or method to another that is widely considered to be an industry standard or best practice. Essentially, _____ provides a snapshot of the performance of your business and helps you understand where you are in relation to a particular standard. The result is often a business case for making changes in order to make improvements.
   a. Benchmarking
   b. Competitive heterogeneity
   c. Complementors
   d. Cost leadership

10. _____ in marketing and strategic management is an assessment of the strengths and weaknesses of current and potential competitors. This analysis provides both an offensive and defensive strategic context through which to identify opportunities and threats. Competitor profiling coalesces all of the relevant sources of _____ into one framework in the support of efficient and effective strategy formulation, implementation, monitoring and adjustment.
    a. 1990 Clean Air Act
    b. Competitor or Competitive Intelligence
    c. 28-hour day
    d. Competitor analysis

11. The general definition of an _____ is an evaluation of a person, organization, system, process, project or product. _____s are performed to ascertain the validity and reliability of information; also to provide an assessment of a system's internal control. The goal of an _____ is to express an opinion on the person / organization/system (etc) in question, under evaluation based on work done on a test basis.

a. Internal control
b. Audit
c. A Stake in the Outcome
d. Audit committee

12. The _____ is a performance management tool for measuring whether the smaller-scale operational activities of a company are aligned with its larger-scale objectives in terms of vision and strategy.

By focusing not only on financial outcomes but also on the operational, marketing and developmental inputs to these, the _____ helps provide a more comprehensive view of a business, which in turn helps organizations act in their best long-term interests. This tool is also being used to address business response to climate change and greenhouse gas emissions.

a. Management development
b. Commercial management
c. Balanced scorecard
d. Middle management

13. In marketing, _____ has come to mean the process by which marketers try to create an image or identity in the minds of their target market for its product, brand, or organization. It is the 'relative competitive comparison' their product occupies in a given market as perceived by the target market.

Re-_____ involves changing the identity of a product, relative to the identity of competing products, in the collective minds of the target market.

a. Positioning
b. Customer analytics
c. PEST analysis
d. Context analysis

14. In economics, _____ is the removal of intermediaries in a supply chain: 'cutting out the middleman'. Instead of going through traditional distribution channels, which had some type of intermediate (such as a distributor, wholesaler, broker, or agent), companies may now deal with every customer directly, for example via the Internet. One important factor is a drop in the cost of servicing customers directly.
a. 28-hour day
b. Virtual enterprise
c. Disintermediation
d. 1990 Clean Air Act

Chapter 8. E-marketing

15. _____ is the self-government of a nation, country or some portion thereof, generally exercising sovereignty.

The term _____ is used in contrast to subjugation, which refers to a region as a 'territory' --subject to the political and military control of an external government. The word is sometimes used in a weaker sense to contrast with hegemony, the indirect control of one nation by another, more powerful nation.

   a. A4e
   b. AAAI
   c. A Stake in the Outcome
   d. Independence

16. _____ is the corporate management term for the act of reorganizing the legal, ownership, operational, or other structures of a company for the purpose of making it more profitable, or better organized for its present needs. Alternate reasons for _____ include a change of ownership or ownership structure, demerger repositioning debt _____ and financial _____.
   a. Market value
   b. Market value added
   c. Restructuring
   d. Net worth

17. _____, in marketing, manufacturing, call centres and management, is the use of flexible computer-aided manufacturing systems to produce custom output. Those systems combine the low unit costs of mass production processes with the flexibility of individual customization.

'_____' is the new frontier in business competition for both manufacturing and service industries.

   a. 28-hour day
   b. Mass customization
   c. 33 Strategies of War
   d. 1990 Clean Air Act

18. _____ is the acquisition of goods and/or services at the best possible total cost of ownership, in the right quality and quantity, at the right time, in the right place and from the right source for the direct benefit or use of corporations, individuals generally via a contract. Simple _____ may involve nothing more than repeat purchasing. Complex _____ could involve finding long term partners - or even 'co-destiny' suppliers that might fundamentally commit one organization to another.

a. Sole proprietorship
b. Procurement
c. Psychological pricing
d. Golden parachute

19. _____ of the learning curve effect and the closely related experience curve effect express the relationship between equations for experience and efficiency or between efficiency gains and investment in the effort. The experience of 'learning curves' was first observed by the 19th Century German psychologist Hermann Ebbinghaus according to the difficulty of memorizing varying numbers of verbal stimuli, and subsequent learning about the complex processes of learning are discussed in the

The rule used for representing the learning curve effect states that the more times a task has been performed, the less time will be required on each subsequent iteration.

a. Distribution
b. Spatial Decision Support Systems
c. Point biserial correlation coefficient
d. Models

20. _____ is one of the four Ps of the marketing mix. The other three aspects are product, promotion, and place. It is also a key variable in microeconomic price allocation theory.
a. Transfer pricing
b. Penetration pricing
c. Price floor
d. Pricing

21. Why do retail stores need _____? With respect to the key objectives of growth and profit for any retail entity, _____ should significantly improve sales margins and increase sales by enabling the vendor to price variably and hence suitably and to control its product range based on profit margins. The retail stores will be able to compete more effectively with rivals in the form of mixed multiples, mail order and online retailers, who are often able to undercut but who do not generally have the same understanding of the retail market. In particular _____ is recognised as encouraging impulse buys, cross-selling of products and repeat sales.
a. Dynamic pricing
b. 28-hour day
c. 33 Strategies of War
d. 1990 Clean Air Act

Chapter 8. E-marketing

22. _____ occurs when manufacturers (brands) disintermediate their channel partners, such as distributors, retailers, dealers, and sales representatives, by selling their products direct to consumers through general marketing methods and/or over the internet through eCommerce.

Some manufacturers want their brands to capture the power of the internet but do not want to create conflict with their other distribution channels, as these partners are necessary and viable for any manufacturer to maintain and gain success. The Census Bureau of the U.S. Department of Commerce reported that online sales in 2005 grew 24.6 percent over 2004 to reach 86.3 billion dollars.

   a. Brand image
   b. Brand loyalty
   c. Brand extension
   d. Channel conflict

23. The _____ captures an expanded spectrum of values and criteria for measuring organizational success: economic, ecological and social. With the ratification of the United Nations and ICLEI _____ standard for urban and community accounting in early 2007, this became the dominant approach to public sector full cost accounting. Similar UN standards apply to natural capital and human capital measurement to assist in measurements required by _____, e.g. the ecoBudget standard for reporting ecological footprint.
   a. 28-hour day
   b. 1990 Clean Air Act
   c. 33 Strategies of War
   d. Triple bottom line

24. A _____ is a name or trademark connected with a product or producer. _____s have become increasingly important components of culture and the economy, now being described as 'cultural accessories and personal philosophies'.

Some people distinguish the psychological aspect of a _____ from the experiential aspect.

   a. Brand awareness
   b. Brand loyalty
   c. Brand extension
   d. Brand

25. In finance, an _____ is a contract between a buyer and a seller that gives the buyer the right--but not the obligation-- to buy or to sell a particular asset (the underlying asset) at a later day at an agreed price. In return for granting the _____, the seller collects a payment (the premium) from the buyer. A call _____ gives the buyer the right to buy the underlying asset; a put _____ gives the buyer of the _____ the right to sell the underlying asset.

a. AAAI
b. A Stake in the Outcome
c. A4e
d. Option

26. _____ is one of the managerial functions like planning, organizing, staffing and directing. It is an important function because it helps to check the errors and to take the corrective action so that deviation from standards are minimized and stated goals of the organization are achieved in desired manner. According to modern concepts, _____ is a foreseeing action whereas earlier concept of _____ was used only when errors were detected. _____ in management means setting standards, measuring actual performance and taking corrective action.
    a. Turnover
    b. Schedule of reinforcement
    c. Control
    d. Decision tree pruning

27. The buzzwords _____ and viral advertising refer to marketing techniques that use pre-existing social networks to produce increases in brand awareness or to achieve other marketing objectives (such as product sales) through self-replicating viral processes, analogous to the spread of pathological and computer viruses. It can be word-of-mouth delivered or enhanced by the network effects of the Internet. Viral promotions may take the form of video clips, interactive Flash games, advergames, ebooks, brandable software, images, or even text messages.
    a. 28-hour day
    b. 33 Strategies of War
    c. Viral marketing
    d. 1990 Clean Air Act

Chapter 9. Customer relationship management

1. The phrase mergers and _____s refers to the aspect of corporate strategy, corporate finance and management dealing with the buying, selling and combining of different companies that can aid, finance, or help a growing company in a given industry grow rapidly without having to create another business entity.

   An _____, also known as a takeover or a buyout, is the buying of one company (the 'target') by another. An _____ may be friendly or hostile.

   a. A4e
   b. Acquisition
   c. A Stake in the Outcome
   d. AAAI

2.

   _____ is a systematic method to improve the 'value' of goods or products and services by using an examination of function. Value, as defined, is the ratio of function to cost. Value can therefore be increased by either improving the function or reducing the cost.

   a. Cellular manufacturing
   b. Value engineering
   c. Capacity planning
   d. Master production schedule

3. _____ is the activity that the selling organization undertakes to reduce customer account defections. The success of this activity is when the customer account places an additional order before a 12-month period has expired. Note that ideally these orders will need to contribute similar financial amounts to the previous 12 months.
   a. Process automation
   b. Customer retention
   c. Business rule
   d. Foreign ownership

4. _____ is an integrated communications-based process through which individuals and communities discover that existing and newly-identified needs and wants may be satisfied by the products and services of others.

   _____ is defined by the American _____ Association as the activity, set of institutions, and processes for creating, communicating, delivering, and exchanging offerings that have value for customers, clients, partners, and society at large. The term developed from the original meaning which referred literally to going to market, as in shopping, or going to a market to buy or sell goods or services.

Chapter 9. Customer relationship management

a. Disruptive technology
b. Market development
c. Customer relationship management
d. Marketing

5. _____, in marketing, manufacturing, call centres and management, is the use of flexible computer-aided manufacturing systems to produce custom output. Those systems combine the low unit costs of mass production processes with the flexibility of individual customization.

'_____' is the new frontier in business competition for both manufacturing and service industries.

a. 33 Strategies of War
b. 28-hour day
c. 1990 Clean Air Act
d. Mass customization

6. In economics, _____ describes the state of a market with respect to competition.

- Perfect competition, in which the market consists of a very large number of firms producing a homogeneous product.
- Monopolistic competition where there are a large number of independent firms which have a very small proportion of the market share.
- Oligopoly, in which a market is dominated by a small number of firms which own more than 40% of the market share.
- Oligopsony, a market dominated by many sellers and a few buyers.
- Monopoly, where there is only one provider of a product or service.
- Natural monopoly, a monopoly in which economies of scale cause efficiency to increase continuously with the size of the firm. A firm is a natural monopoly if it is able to serve the entire market demand at a lower cost than any combination of two or more smaller, more specialized firms.
- Monopsony, when there is only one buyer in a market.

The imperfectly competitive structure is quite identical to the realistic market conditions where some monopolistic competitors, monopolists, oligopolists, and duopolists exist and dominate the market conditions. The elements of _____ include the number and size distribution of firms, entry conditions, and the extent of differentiation.

These somewhat abstract concerns tend to determine some but not all details of a specific concrete market system where buyers and sellers actually meet and commit to trade.

a. Deflation
b. Leading indicator
c. Productivity management
d. Market structure

Chapter 9. Customer relationship management

7. _____s (or MarCom or Integrated _____s) are messages and related media used to communicate with a market. Those who practice advertising, branding, direct marketing, graphic design, marketing, packaging, promotion, publicity, sponsorship, public relations, sales, sales promotion and online marketing are termed marketing communicators, _____ managers, or more briefly as marcom managers.

Traditionally, _____ practitioners focus on the creation and execution of printed marketing collateral; however, academic and professional research developed the practice to use strategic elements of branding and marketing in order to ensure consistency of message delivery throughout an organization.

   a. Adam Smith
   b. Marketing communication
   c. Thomas Dale DeLay
   d. Abraham Harold Maslow

8. _____ is a form of communication that typically attempts to persuade potential customers to purchase or to consume more of a particular brand of product or service. 'While now central to the contemporary global economy and the reproduction of global production networks, it is only quite recently that _____ has been more than a marginal influence on patterns of sales and production. The formation of modern _____ was intimately bound up with the emergence of new forms of monopoly capitalism around the end of the 19th and beginning of the 20th century as one element in corporate strategies to create, organize and where possible control markets, especially for mass produced consumer goods.
   a. Advertising
   b. AAAI
   c. A Stake in the Outcome
   d. A4e

9. In economics, business, retail, and accounting, a _____ is the value of money that has been used up to produce something, and hence is not available for use anymore. In economics, a _____ is an alternative that is given up as a result of a decision. In business, the _____ may be one of acquisition, in which case the amount of money expended to acquire it is counted as _____.
   a. Cost overrun
   b. Fixed costs
   c. Cost
   d. Cost allocation

10. The _____ is an abstract description for layered communications and computer network protocol design. It was developed as part of the Open Systems Interconnection (OSI) initiative. In its most basic form, it divides network architecture into seven layers which, from top to bottom, are the Application, Presentation, Session, Transport, Network, Data-Link, and Physical Layers.

Chapter 9. Customer relationship management 55

a. AAAI
b. A4e
c. A Stake in the Outcome
d. Open Systems Interconnection Reference Model

11. A _____ is a type of business entity in which partners (owners) share with each other the profits or losses of the business. _____s are often favored over corporations for taxation purposes, as the _____ structure does not generally incur a tax on profits before it is distributed to the partners (i.e. there is no dividend tax levied.) However, depending on the _____ structure and the jurisdiction in which it operates, owners of a _____ may be exposed to greater personal liability than they would as shareholders of a corporation.

a. Due process
b. Mediation
c. Federal Employers Liability Act
d. Partnership

12. _____ systems are rule-based systems that are able to automatically provide solutions to repetitive management problems (Turban, Leidner, McLean and Wetherbe, 2007.) _____s are very closely related to business informatics and business analytics.

_____ systems are based on business rules.

a. Efficient Consumer Response
b. Executive development
c. Entertainment Management
d. Automated decision support

13. In finance, an _____ is a contract between a buyer and a seller that gives the buyer the right--but not the obligation--to buy or to sell a particular asset (the underlying asset) at a later day at an agreed price. In return for granting the _____, the seller collects a payment (the premium) from the buyer. A call _____ gives the buyer the right to buy the underlying asset; a put _____ gives the buyer of the _____ the right to sell the underlying asset.

a. A Stake in the Outcome
b. A4e
c. Option
d. AAAI

14. _____ is an advertisement in which a particular product specifically mentions a competitor by name for the express purpose of showing why the competitor is inferior to the product naming it.

Chapter 9. Customer relationship management

This should not be confused with parody advertisements, where a fictional product is being advertised for the purpose of poking fun at the particular advertisement, nor should it be confused with the use of a coined brand name for the purpose of comparing the product without actually naming an actual competitor. ('Wikipedia tastes better and is less filling than the Encyclopedia Galactica.')

In the 1980s, during what has been referred to as the cola wars, soft-drink manufacturer Pepsi ran a series of advertisements where people, caught on hidden camera, in a blind taste test, chose Pepsi over rival Coca-Cola.

   a. 1990 Clean Air Act
   b. 28-hour day
   c. 33 Strategies of War
   d. Comparative advertising

15. _____ is the process of filtering for information or patterns using techniques involving collaboration among multiple agents, viewpoints, data sources, etc. Applications of _____ typically involve very large data sets. _____ methods have been applied to many different kinds of data including sensing and monitoring data - such as in mineral exploration, environmental sensing over large areas or multiple sensors; financial data - such as financial service institutions that integrate many financial sources; or in electronic commerce and web 2.0 applications where the focus is on user data, etc.
   a. 28-hour day
   b. 33 Strategies of War
   c. Collaborative filtering
   d. 1990 Clean Air Act

16. An _____ is a private network that uses Internet protocols, network connectivity, and possibly the public telecommunication system to securely share part of an organization's information or operations with suppliers, vendors, partners, customers or other businesses. An _____ can be viewed as part of a company's intranet that is extended to users outside the company (e.g.: normally over the Internet.) It has also been described as a 'state of mind' in which the Internet is perceived as a way to do business with a preapproved set of other companies business-to-business (B2B), in isolation from all other Internet users.
   a. AAAI
   b. A4e
   c. Extranet
   d. A Stake in the Outcome

Chapter 9. Customer relationship management

17. _____ is a strategic planning method used to evaluate the Strengths, Weaknesses, Opportunities, and Threats involved in a project or in a business venture. It involves specifying the objective of the business venture or project and identifying the internal and external factors that are favorable and unfavorable to achieving that objective. The technique is credited to Albert Humphrey, who led a convention at Stanford University in the 1960s and 1970s using data from Fortune 500 companies.
   a. Corporate image
   b. Market share
   c. Marketing
   d. SWOT analysis

18. _____ consists of the mental process of thinking involved with the process of judging the merits of multiple options and selecting one of them for action. Some simple examples include deciding whether to get up in the morning or go back to sleep, or selecting a given route for a journey. More complex examples (often decisions that affect what a person thinks or their core beliefs) include choosing a lifestyle, religious affiliation, or political position.
   a. Championship mobilization
   b. Groups decision making
   c. Trade study
   d. Choice

Chapter 10. Change management

1. _____ is a structured approach to transitioning individuals, teams, and organizations from a current state to a desired future state. The current definition of _____ includes both organizational _____ processes and individual _____ models, which together are used to manage the people side of change.

A number of models are available for understanding the transitioning of individuals through the phases of _____ and strengthening organizational development initiative in both government and corporate sectors.

   a. 33 Strategies of War
   b. 28-hour day
   c. 1990 Clean Air Act
   d. Change management

2. _____, commonly known as e-commerce, consists of the buying and selling of products or services over electronic systems such as the Internet and other computer networks. The amount of trade conducted electronically has grown extraordinarily with widespread Internet usage. The use of commerce is conducted in this way, spurring and drawing on innovations in electronic funds transfer, supply chain management, Internet marketing, online transaction processing, electronic data interchange (EDI), inventory management systems, and automated data collection systems.
   a. A4e
   b. A Stake in the Outcome
   c. Online shopping
   d. Electronic Commerce

3. A _____ or business method is a collection of related, structured activities or tasks that produce a specific service or product (serve a particular goal) for a particular customer or customers. It often can be visualized with a flowchart as a sequence of activities.

There are three types of _____es:

   1. Management processes, the processes that govern the operation of a system. Typical management processes include 'Corporate Governance' and 'Strategic Management'.
   2. Operational processes, processes that constitute the core business and create the primary value stream. Typical operational processes are Purchasing, Manufacturing, Marketing, and Sales.
   3. Supporting processes, which support the core processes. Examples include Accounting, Recruitment, Technical support.

A _____ begins with a customer's need and ends with a customer's need fulfillment. Process oriented organizations break down the barriers of structural departments and try to avoid functional silos.

Chapter 10. Change management

a. Business process
b. 33 Strategies of War
c. 1990 Clean Air Act
d. 28-hour day

4. _____ is a systematic approach to help any organization optimize its underlying processes to achieve more efficient results.

The organization may be a for-profit business, a non-profit organization, a government agency, or any other ongoing concern. Most _____ techniques were developed and refined in the manufacturing era, though many of the methodologies (like Six Sigma) have been successfully adapted to work in the predominantly service-based economy of today.

a. Contingency theory
b. Business process improvement
c. Micromanagement
d. Fix it twice

5. In organizational development (OD), _____ is a series of actions taken by a Process Owner to identify, analyze and improve existing processes within an organization to meet new goals and objectives. These actions often follow a specific methodology or strategy to create successful results. A sampling of these are listed below.

a. Process improvement
b. Letter of resignation
c. Product innovation
d. Supervisory board

6. _____ refers to the movement of cash into or out of a business or financial product. It is usually measured during a specified, finite period of time. Measurement of _____ can be used

- to determine a project's rate of return or value. The time of _____s into and out of projects are used as inputs in financial models such as internal rate of return, and net present value.
- to determine problems with a business's liquidity. Being profitable does not necessarily mean being liquid. A company can fail because of a shortage of cash, even while profitable.
- as an alternate measure of a business's profits when it is believed that accrual accounting concepts do not represent economic realities. For example, a company may be notionally profitable but generating little operational cash (as may be the case for a company that barters its products rather than selling for cash.) In such a case, the company may be deriving additional operating cash by issuing shares evaluating default risk, re-investment requirements, etc.

_____ is a generic term used differently depending on the context. It may be defined by users for their own purposes.

a. Gross profit
b. Gross profit margin
c. Sweat equity
d. Cash flow

7. _____ is the discipline of planning, organizing and managing resources to bring about the successful completion of specific project goals and objectives. It is often closely related to and sometimes conflated with Program management.

A project is a finite endeavor--having specific start and completion dates--undertaken to meet particular goals and objectives, usually to bring about beneficial change or added value.

a. Precedence diagram
b. Work package
c. Project engineer
d. Project management

8. _____, commonly referred to as 'eBusiness' or 'e-Business', may be defined as the utilization of information and communication technologies (ICT) in support of all the activities of business. Commerce constitutes the exchange of products and services between businesses, groups and individuals and hence can be seen as one of the essential activities of any business. Hence, electronic commerce or eCommerce focuses on the use of ICT to enable the external activities and relationships of the business with individuals, groups and other businesses.

a. A4e
b. A Stake in the Outcome
c. AAAI
d. Electronic business

9. _____ is a strategic planning method used to evaluate the Strengths, Weaknesses, Opportunities, and Threats involved in a project or in a business venture. It involves specifying the objective of the business venture or project and identifying the internal and external factors that are favorable and unfavorable to achieving that objective. The technique is credited to Albert Humphrey, who led a convention at Stanford University in the 1960s and 1970s using data from Fortune 500 companies.

a. Corporate image
b. Marketing
c. Market share
d. SWOT analysis

Chapter 10. Change management

10. _____ refers to the process of screening, and selecting qualified people for a job at an organization or firm mid- and large-size organizations and companies often retain professional recruiters or outsource some of the process to _____ agencies. External _____ is the process of attracting and selecting employees from outside the organization.

The _____ industry has four main types of agencies: employment agencies, _____ websites and job search engines, 'headhunters' for executive and professional _____, and in-house _____.

   a. Referral recruitment
   b. Recruitment
   c. Labour hire
   d. Recruitment Process Outsourcing

11. The _____ is an abstract description for layered communications and computer network protocol design. It was developed as part of the Open Systems Interconnection (OSI) initiative. In its most basic form, it divides network architecture into seven layers which, from top to bottom, are the Application, Presentation, Session, Transport, Network, Data-Link, and Physical Layers.
   a. A4e
   b. A Stake in the Outcome
   c. AAAI
   d. Open Systems Interconnection Reference Model

12. _____ is subcontracting a process, such as product design or manufacturing, to a third-party company. The decision to outsource is often made in the interest of lowering cost or making better use of time and energy costs, redirecting or conserving energy directed at the competencies of a particular business, or to make more efficient use of land, labor, capital, (information) technology and resources. _____ became part of the business lexicon during the 1980s.
   a. Opinion leadership
   b. Outsourcing
   c. Operant conditioning
   d. Unemployment insurance

13. An _____ is a mostly hierarchical concept of subordination of entities that collaborate and contribute to serve one common aim.

Organizations are a variant of clustered entities. The structure of an organization is usually set up in many a styles, dependent on their objectives and ambience.

Chapter 10. Change management

a. Informal organization
b. Open shop
c. Organizational development
d. Organizational structure

14. _____ of the learning curve effect and the closely related experience curve effect express the relationship between equations for experience and efficiency or between efficiency gains and investment in the effort. The experience of 'learning curves' was first observed by the 19th Century German psychologist Hermann Ebbinghaus according to the difficulty of memorizing varying numbers of verbal stimuli, and subsequent learning about the complex processes of learning are discussed in the

.

The rule used for representing the learning curve effect states that the more times a task has been performed, the less time will be required on each subsequent iteration.

a. Models
b. Distribution
c. Point biserial correlation coefficient
d. Spatial Decision Support Systems

15. _____ is generally a team of individuals at the highest level of organizational management who have the day-to-day responsibilities of managing a corporation. There are most often higher levels of responsibility, such as a board of directors and those who own the company (shareholders), but they focus on managing the _____ instead of the day-to-day activities of the business.

They are sometimes referred to, within corporations, as top management, upper management, higher management, or simply seniors.

a. Management development
b. Functional management
c. Crisis management
d. Senior management

16. _____ is an idea in the field of Organizational studies and management which describes the psychology, attitudes, experiences, beliefs and Values (personal and cultural values) of an organization. It has been defined as 'the specific collection of values and norms that are shared by people and groups in an organization and that control the way they interact with each other and with stakeholders outside the organization.'

Chapter 10. Change management

This definition continues to explain organizational values also known as 'beliefs and ideas about what kinds of goals members of an organization should pursue and ideas about the appropriate kinds or standards of behavior organizational members should use to achieve these goals. From organizational values develop organizational norms, guidelines or expectations that prescribe appropriate kinds of behavior by employees in particular situations and control the behavior of organizational members towards one another.'

_____ is not the same as corporate culture.

a. Union shop
b. Organizational culture
c. Organizational effectiveness
d. Organizational development

17. _____ comprises a range of practices used in an organisation to identify, create, represent, distribute and enable adoption of insights and experiences. Such insights and experiences comprise knowledge, either embodied in individuals or embedded in organisational processes or practice.

An established discipline since 1991 , _____ includes courses taught in the fields of business administration, information systems, management, and library and information sciences .

a. 28-hour day
b. 1990 Clean Air Act
c. 33 Strategies of War
d. Knowledge management

18. In decision theory and estimation theory, the _____ of an estimator, $\hat{\theta}$, of an unknown parameter of the distribution, θ, is the expected value of the loss function

$$R(\theta, \hat{\theta}) = \mathbb{E}_\theta L(\theta, \hat{\theta}) = \int L(\theta, \hat{\theta})\, dP_\theta.$$

where dP_θ is a probability measure parametrized by θ.

- For a scalar parameter θ and a quadratic loss function,

$$L(\theta, \hat{\theta}) = (\theta - \hat{\theta})^2$$

the _____ function becomes the mean squared error of the estimate,

$$R(\theta, \hat{\theta}) = E_\theta (\theta - \hat{\theta})^2$$

- In density estimation, the unknown parameter is probability density itself. The loss function is typically chosen to be a norm in an appropriate function space. For example, for L^2 norm,

$$L(f, \hat{f}) = \|f - \hat{f}\|_2^2$$

the _____ function becomes the mean integrated squared error

$$R(f, \hat{f}) = E\|f - \hat{f}\|^2$$

a. Linear model
b. Financial modeling
c. Risk aversion
d. Risk

19. _____ is the identification, assessment, and prioritization of risks followed by coordinated and economical application of resources to minimize, monitor, and control the probability and/or impact of unfortunate events.. Risks can come from uncertainty in financial markets, project failures, legal liabilities, credit risk, accidents, natural causes and disasters as well as deliberate attacks from an adversary. Several _____ standards have been developed including the Project Management Institute, the National Institute of Science and Technology, actuarial societies, and ISO standards.
a. Risk management
b. Succession planning
c. Trademark
d. Kanban

Chapter 11. Analysis and design

1. A _____ is a depiction of a sequence of operations, declared as work of a person, a group of persons, an organization of staff, or one or more simple or complex mechanisms. _____ may be seen as any abstraction of real work, segregated in workshare, work split or other types of ordering. For control purposes, _____ may be a view on real work under a chosen aspect, thus serving as a virtual representation of actual work.
   a. Workflow
   b. Resource-based view
   c. Management development
   d. Time management

2. _____ is a strategic planning method used to evaluate the Strengths, Weaknesses, Opportunities, and Threats involved in a project or in a business venture. It involves specifying the objective of the business venture or project and identifying the internal and external factors that are favorable and unfavorable to achieving that objective. The technique is credited to Albert Humphrey, who led a convention at Stanford University in the 1960s and 1970s using data from Fortune 500 companies.
   a. SWOT analysis
   b. Marketing
   c. Corporate image
   d. Market share

3. _____ is the analysis of how a task is accomplished, including a detailed description of both manual and mental activities, task and element durations, task frequency, task allocation, task complexity, environmental conditions, necessary clothing and equipment, and any other unique factors involved in or required for one or more people to perform a given task. _____ emerged from research in applied behavior analysis and still has considerable research in that area.

   Information from a _____ can then be used for many purposes, such as personnel selection and training, tool or equipment design, procedure design (e.g., design of checklists or decision support systems) and automation.

   a. 28-hour day
   b. 33 Strategies of War
   c. Task analysis
   d. 1990 Clean Air Act

4. A _____ is an alliance among individuals or groups, during which they cooperate in joint action, each in his own self-interest, joining forces together for a common cause. This alliance may be temporary or a matter of convenience. A _____ thus differs from a more formal covenant.

Chapter 11. Analysis and design

a. 33 Strategies of War
b. Coalition
c. 1990 Clean Air Act
d. 28-hour day

5. The term _____ is used in various contexts. For example, in business process modeling the enterprise _____ is often referred to as the business _____. Process models are core concepts in the discipline of Process Engineering.

a. 33 Strategies of War
b. 1990 Clean Air Act
c. 28-hour day
d. Process model

6.

_____ is a systematic method to improve the 'value' of goods or products and services by using an examination of function. Value, as defined, is the ratio of function to cost. Value can therefore be increased by either improving the function or reducing the cost.

a. Value engineering
b. Master production schedule
c. Cellular manufacturing
d. Capacity planning

7. _____ is a strategic planning method that some organizations use to make flexible long-term plans. It is in large part an adaptation and generalization of classic methods used by military intelligence.

The original method was that a group of analysts would generate simulation games for policy makers. In business applications, the emphasis on gaming the behavior of opponents was reduced (shifting more toward a game against nature). At Royal Dutch/Shell for example, _____ was viewed as changing mindsets about the exogenous part of the world, prior to formulating specific strategies.

a. Time and attendance
b. Labour productivity
c. Retroactive overtime
d. Scenario planning

8. _____ is an advertisement in which a particular product specifically mentions a competitor by name for the express purpose of showing why the competitor is inferior to the product naming it.

This should not be confused with parody advertisements, where a fictional product is being advertised for the purpose of poking fun at the particular advertisement, nor should it be confused with the use of a coined brand name for the purpose of comparing the product without actually naming an actual competitor. ('Wikipedia tastes better and is less filling than the Encyclopedia Galactica.')

In the 1980s, during what has been referred to as the cola wars, soft-drink manufacturer Pepsi ran a series of advertisements where people, caught on hidden camera, in a blind taste test, chose Pepsi over rival Coca-Cola.

   a. 1990 Clean Air Act
   b. 33 Strategies of War
   c. 28-hour day
   d. Comparative advertising

9. The _____ is an abstract description for layered communications and computer network protocol design. It was developed as part of the Open Systems Interconnection (OSI) initiative. In its most basic form, it divides network architecture into seven layers which, from top to bottom, are the Application, Presentation, Session, Transport, Network, Data-Link, and Physical Layers.
   a. A Stake in the Outcome
   b. A4e
   c. AAAI
   d. Open Systems Interconnection Reference Model

10. _____ refers to the practice of making websites usable by people of all abilities and disabilities. When sites are correctly designed, developed and edited, all users can have equal access to information and functionality. For example, when a site is coded with semantically meaningful HTML, with textual equivalents provided for images and with links named meaningfully, this helps blind users using text-to-speech software and/or text-to-Braille hardware.
   a. Web accessibility
   b. 33 Strategies of War
   c. 28-hour day
   d. 1990 Clean Air Act

11. The _____ captures an expanded spectrum of values and criteria for measuring organizational success: economic, ecological and social. With the ratification of the United Nations and ICLEI _____ standard for urban and community accounting in early 2007, this became the dominant approach to public sector full cost accounting. Similar UN standards apply to natural capital and human capital measurement to assist in measurements required by _____, e.g. the ecoBudget standard for reporting ecological footprint.

Chapter 11. Analysis and design

  a. 1990 Clean Air Act
  b. 28-hour day
  c. 33 Strategies of War
  d. Triple bottom line

12. A _____ is typically described as a deliberate plan of action to guide decisions and achieve rational outcome(s.) However, the term may also be used to denote what is actually done, even though it is unplanned.

The term may apply to government, private sector organizations and groups, and individuals.

  a. 1990 Clean Air Act
  b. 33 Strategies of War
  c. Policy
  d. 28-hour day

13. In business and accounting, _____s are everything of value that is owned by a person or company. Any property or object of value that one possesses, usually considered as applicable to the payment of one's debts is considered an _____. Simplistically stated, _____s are things of value that can be readily converted into cash.
  a. AAAI
  b. A4e
  c. A Stake in the Outcome
  d. Asset

14. _____, commonly known as e-commerce, consists of the buying and selling of products or services over electronic systems such as the Internet and other computer networks. The amount of trade conducted electronically has grown extraordinarily with widespread Internet usage. The use of commerce is conducted in this way, spurring and drawing on innovations in electronic funds transfer, supply chain management, Internet marketing, online transaction processing, electronic data interchange (EDI), inventory management systems, and automated data collection systems.
  a. A4e
  b. Online shopping
  c. A Stake in the Outcome
  d. Electronic Commerce

Chapter 12. Implementation and maintenance

1. _____, commonly referred to as 'eBusiness' or 'e-Business', may be defined as the utilization of information and communication technologies (ICT) in support of all the activities of business. Commerce constitutes the exchange of products and services between businesses, groups and individuals and hence can be seen as one of the essential activities of any business. Hence, electronic commerce or eCommerce focuses on the use of ICT to enable the external activities and relationships of the business with individuals, groups and other businesses .
   a. A4e
   b. AAAI
   c. A Stake in the Outcome
   d. Electronic business

2. In decision theory and estimation theory, the _____ of an estimator, $\hat{\theta}$, of an unknown parameter of the distribution, θ, is the expected value of the loss function

$$R(\theta, \hat{\theta}) = \mathbb{E}_\theta L(\theta, \hat{\theta}) = \int L(\theta, \hat{\theta}) \, dP_\theta.$$

where dP_θ is a probability measure parametrized by θ.

- For a scalar parameter θ and a quadratic loss function,

$$L(\theta, \hat{\theta}) = (\theta - \hat{\theta})^2$$

the _____ function becomes the mean squared error of the estimate,

$$R(\theta, \hat{\theta}) = E_\theta (\theta - \hat{\theta})^2$$

- In density estimation, the unknown parameter is probability density itself. The loss function is typically chosen to be a norm in an appropriate function space. For example, for L^2 norm,

$$L(f, \hat{f}) = \|f - \hat{f}\|_2^2$$

the _____ function becomes the mean integrated squared error

$$R(f, \hat{f}) = E\|f - \hat{f}\|^2$$

Chapter 12. Implementation and maintenance

a. Risk aversion
b. Financial modeling
c. Linear model
d. Risk

3. _____ is the identification, assessment, and prioritization of risks followed by coordinated and economical application of resources to minimize, monitor, and control the probability and/or impact of unfortunate events.. Risks can come from uncertainty in financial markets, project failures, legal liabilities, credit risk, accidents, natural causes and disasters as well as deliberate attacks from an adversary. Several _____ standards have been developed including the Project Management Institute, the National Institute of Science and Technology, actuarial societies, and ISO standards.

a. Kanban
b. Succession planning
c. Trademark
d. Risk management

4. The _____ is an abstract description for layered communications and computer network protocol design. It was developed as part of the Open Systems Interconnection (OSI) initiative. In its most basic form, it divides network architecture into seven layers which, from top to bottom, are the Application, Presentation, Session, Transport, Network, Data-Link, and Physical Layers.

a. A Stake in the Outcome
b. A4e
c. AAAI
d. Open Systems Interconnection Reference Model

5. _____ is a strategic planning method used to evaluate the Strengths, Weaknesses, Opportunities, and Threats involved in a project or in a business venture. It involves specifying the objective of the business venture or project and identifying the internal and external factors that are favorable and unfavorable to achieving that objective. The technique is credited to Albert Humphrey, who led a convention at Stanford University in the 1960s and 1970s using data from Fortune 500 companies.

a. Corporate image
b. Market share
c. Marketing
d. SWOT analysis

6. 'Speaking generally, properties are those physical quantities which directly describe the physical attributes of the system; _____s are those combinations of the properties which suffice to determine the response of the system. Properties can have all sorts of dimensions, depending upon the system being considered; _____s are dimensionless, or have the dimension of time or its reciprocal.'

The term can also be used in engineering contexts, however, as it is typically used in the physical sciences.

When the terms formal _____ and actual _____ are used, they generally correspond with the definitions used in computer science.

   a. Parameter
   b. 33 Strategies of War
   c. 1990 Clean Air Act
   d. 28-hour day

7. A _____ is a graphic representation of the maturity, adoption and business application of specific technologies. The term was coined by Gartner, an analyst/research house, based in the United States, that provides opinions, advice and data on the global information technology industry.

Since 1995, Gartner has used _____s to characterize the over-enthusiasm or 'hype' and subsequent disappointment that typically happens with the introduction of new technologies.

   a. 1990 Clean Air Act
   b. 28-hour day
   c. Hype cycle
   d. 33 Strategies of War

8. An _____ is a private computer network that uses Internet technologies to securely share any part of an organization's information or operational systems with its employees. Sometimes the term refers only to the organization's internal website, but often it is a more extensive part of the organization's computer infrastructure and private websites are an important component and focal point of internal communication and collaboration.

An _____ is built from the same concepts and technologies used for the Internet, such as client-server computing and the Internet Protocol Suite (TCP/IP.)

   a. AAAI
   b. A4e
   c. A Stake in the Outcome
   d. Intranet

9. _____ is an advertisement in which a particular product specifically mentions a competitor by name for the express purpose of showing why the competitor is inferior to the product naming it.

Chapter 12. Implementation and maintenance

This should not be confused with parody advertisements, where a fictional product is being advertised for the purpose of poking fun at the particular advertisement, nor should it be confused with the use of a coined brand name for the purpose of comparing the product without actually naming an actual competitor. ('Wikipedia tastes better and is less filling than the Encyclopedia Galactica.')

In the 1980s, during what has been referred to as the cola wars, soft-drink manufacturer Pepsi ran a series of advertisements where people, caught on hidden camera, in a blind taste test, chose Pepsi over rival Coca-Cola.

   a. 28-hour day
   b. 1990 Clean Air Act
   c. 33 Strategies of War
   d. Comparative advertising

10. _____ in its literal sense is the process of transformation of local or regional phenomena into global ones. It can be described as a process by which the people of the world are unified into a single society and function together.

This process is a combination of economic, technological, sociocultural and political forces.

   a. Globalization
   b. Histogram
   c. Cost Management
   d. Collaborative Planning, Forecasting and Replenishment

11. _____ is the process whereby an organization establishes the parameters within which programs, investments, and acquisitions are reaching the desired results. Performance Reference Model of the Federal Enterprise Architecture, 2005.

This process of measuring performance often requires the use of statistical evidence to determine progress toward specific defined organizational objectives.

There are many types of measurements.

   a. Performance measurement
   b. CIFMS
   c. Workflow
   d. Crisis management

Chapter 12. Implementation and maintenance

12. _____ is the measurement, collection, analysis and reporting of internet data for purposes of understanding and optimizing web usage.

There are two categories of _____; off-site and on-site _____.

Off-site _____ refers to web measurement and analysis irrespective of whether you own or maintain a website. On-site _____ measure a visitor's journey once on your website.

a. 28-hour day
b. 1990 Clean Air Act
c. 33 Strategies of War
d. Web analytics

13. _____ is an integrated communications-based process through which individuals and communities discover that existing and newly-identified needs and wants may be satisfied by the products and services of others.

_____ is defined by the American _____ Association as the activity, set of institutions, and processes for creating, communicating, delivering, and exchanging offerings that have value for customers, clients, partners, and society at large. The term developed from the original meaning which referred literally to going to market, as in shopping, or going to a market to buy or sell goods or services.

a. Disruptive technology
b. Customer relationship management
c. Market development
d. Marketing

14. _____ is a forward looking process for setting goals and regularly checking progress toward achieving those goals. It is a continual feedback process whereby the actual outputs are measured and compared with the desired goals. Any discrepancy or gap is then fed back into changing the inputs of the process, so as to achieve the desired goals or outputs.

a. 33 Strategies of War
b. 28-hour day
c. Performance management
d. 1990 Clean Air Act

15.

_____ is a systematic method to improve the 'value' of goods or products and services by using an examination of function. Value, as defined, is the ratio of function to cost. Value can therefore be increased by either improving the function or reducing the cost.

   a. Cellular manufacturing
   b. Capacity planning
   c. Value engineering
   d. Master production schedule

16. In game theory, an _____ is a set of moves or strategies taken by the players, or their payoffs resulting from the actions or strategies taken by all players. The two are complementary in that given knowledge of the set of strategies of all players, the final state of the game is known, as are any relevant payoffs. In a game where chance or a random event is involved, the _____ is not known from only the set of strategies, but is only realized when the random event(s) are realized.
   a. AAAI
   b. Outcome
   c. A Stake in the Outcome
   d. A4e

17. In the fields of science, engineering, industry and statistics, _____ is the degree of closeness of a measured or calculated quantity to its actual (true) value. _____ is closely related to precision, also called reproducibility or repeatability, the degree to which further measurements or calculations show the same or similar results. _____ indicates proximity to the true value, precision to the repeatability or reproducibility of the measurement

The results of calculations or a measurement can be accurate but not precise, precise but not accurate, neither, or both.

   a. A Stake in the Outcome
   b. A4e
   c. AAAI
   d. Accuracy

18. In economics, business, retail, and accounting, a _____ is the value of money that has been used up to produce something, and hence is not available for use anymore. In economics, a _____ is an alternative that is given up as a result of a decision. In business, the _____ may be one of acquisition, in which case the amount of money expended to acquire it is counted as _____.

a. Cost allocation
b. Cost
c. Cost overrun
d. Fixed costs

Chapter 1
1. d   2. d   3. d   4. c   5. b   6. d   7. d   8. d   9. a   10. d
11. a   12. d   13. d   14. d   15. d   16. c

Chapter 2
1. c   2. d   3. a   4. a   5. a   6. a   7. b   8. b   9. a   10. a
11. b   12. d   13. d   14. c   15. d   16. c   17. d

Chapter 3
1. d   2. c   3. a   4. d   5. d   6. d   7. d   8. b   9. d   10. d
11. c   12. c   13. d   14. d   15. a   16. c   17. b   18. d   19. b

Chapter 4
1. d   2. d   3. a   4. d   5. b   6. d   7. d   8. d   9. b   10. a
11. c   12. d   13. b   14. d   15. a   16. b   17. a   18. d   19. c   20. d
21. d   22. d

Chapter 5
1. b   2. a   3. d   4. c   5. a   6. a   7. d   8. c   9. d   10. b
11. d   12. d   13. a   14. c   15. a   16. b   17. d   18. b   19. d   20. b
21. b   22. d   23. c   24. a   25. c   26. d   27. c   28. c   29. a   30. c
31. a

Chapter 6
1. a   2. d   3. b   4. c   5. a   6. d   7. b   8. c   9. a   10. b
11. a   12. d   13. c   14. c   15. c   16. c   17. d

Chapter 7
1. d   2. d   3. b   4. c

Chapter 8
1. c   2. c   3. a   4. b   5. d   6. d   7. c   8. b   9. a   10. d
11. b   12. c   13. a   14. c   15. d   16. c   17. b   18. b   19. d   20. d
21. a   22. d   23. d   24. d   25. d   26. c   27. c

Chapter 9
1. b   2. b   3. b   4. d   5. d   6. d   7. b   8. a   9. c   10. d
11. d   12. d   13. c   14. d   15. c   16. c   17. d   18. d

Chapter 10
1. d   2. d   3. a   4. b   5. a   6. d   7. d   8. d   9. d   10. b
11. d   12. b   13. d   14. a   15. d   16. b   17. d   18. d   19. a

Chapter 11
1. a   2. a   3. c   4. b   5. d   6. a   7. d   8. d   9. d   10. a
11. d   12. c   13. d   14. d

ANSWER KEY

Chapter 12
1. d   2. d   3. d   4. d   5. d   6. a   7. c   8. d   9. d   10. a
11. a   12. d   13. d   14. c   15. c   16. b   17. d   18. b

www.ingramcontent.com/pod-product-compliance
Lightning Source LLC
Chambersburg PA
CBHW081849230426
43669CB00018B/2878